P9-DEJ-195

Colombia

Colombia

BY NEL YOMTOV

Enchantment of the World™
Second Series

CHILDREN'S PRESS®

An Imprint of Scholastic Inc.

New York   Toronto   London   Auckland   Sydney
Mexico City   New Delhi   Hong Kong
Danbury, Connecticut

**Cuyahoga Falls
Library**
Cuyahoga Falls, Ohio

Frontispiece: **Independence Day festivities**

Consultant: Ann Farnsworth-Alvear, Associate Professor of History, University of Pennsylvania, Philadelphia, Pennsylvania

Please note: All statistics are as up-to-date as possible at the time of publication.

Book production by The Design Lab

Library of Congress Cataloging-in-Publication Data
Yomtov, Nelson.
 Colombia / by Nel Yomtov.
 pages cm. — (Enchantment of the world, second series)
 Includes bibliographical references and index.
 ISBN 978-0-531-22013-9 (lib. bdg.)
 1. Colombia—Juvenile literature. I. Title.
 F2258.5.Y66 2014
 986.1—dc23   2013026060

No part of this publication may be reproduced in whole or in part, or stored in a retrieval system, or transmitted in any form or by any means, electronic, mechanical, photocopying, recording, or otherwise, without written permission of the publisher. For information regarding permission, write to Scholastic Inc., 557 Broadway, New York, NY 10012.

© 2014 by Scholastic Inc.
All rights reserved. Published in 2014 by Children's Press, an imprint of Scholastic Inc.
Printed in the United States of America 141
SCHOLASTIC, CHILDREN'S PRESS, and associated logos are trademarks and/or registered trademarks of Scholastic Inc.

1 2 3 4 5 6 7 8 9 10 R 23 22 21 20 19 18 17 16 15 14

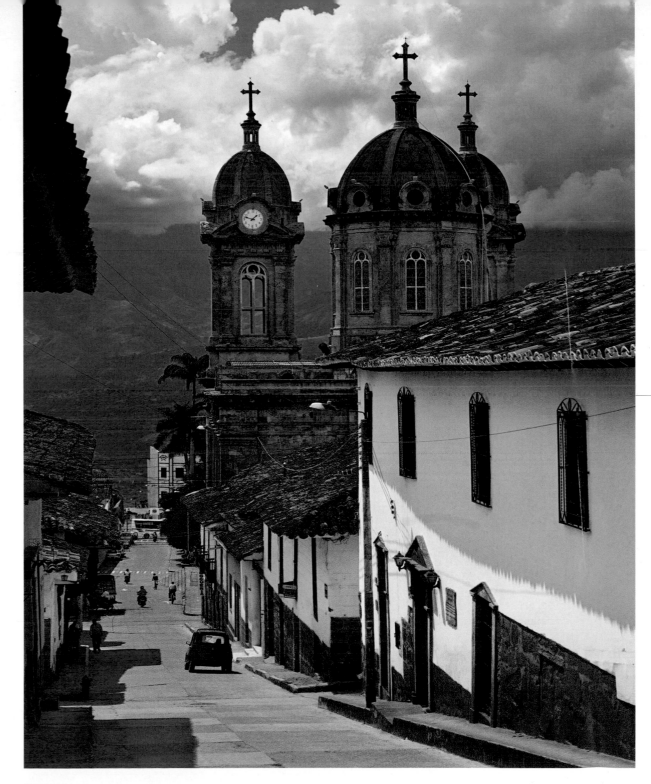

Socorro

Contents

Left to right: **Bridge between Caribbean Islands, schoolchildren, family on motorcycle, boating, grandmother and child**

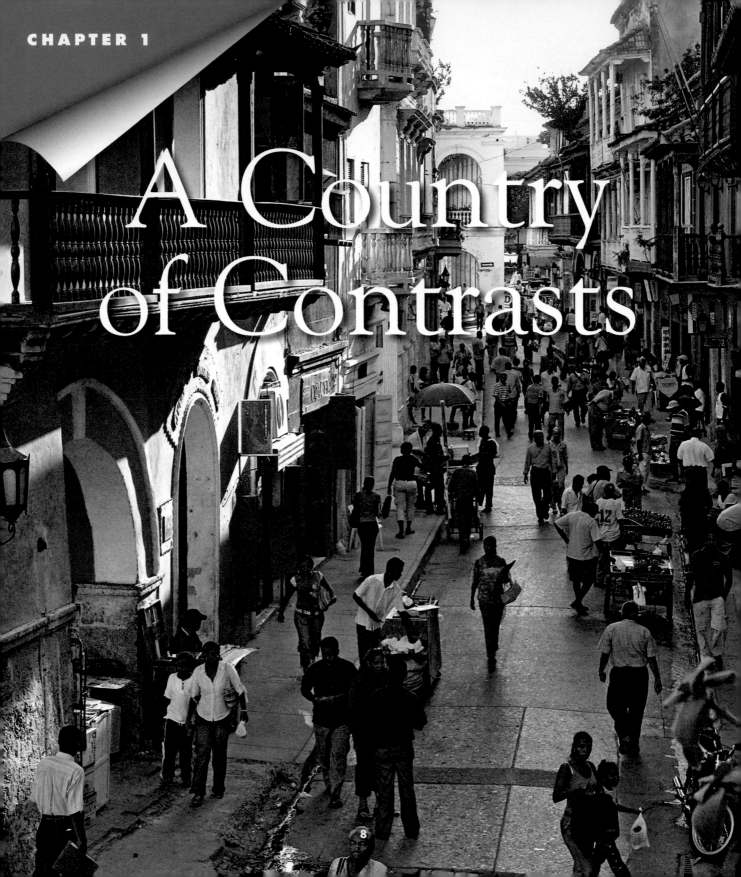

CHAPTER 1

A Country of Contrasts

COLOMBIA IS BLESSED WITH BEAUTY AND DIVERSITY. Located at the northern end of South America, it is the second most biologically diverse country on Earth, second only to Brazil. It is home to roughly 14 percent of all the world's species of plants and animals. Colombia's dazzling range of scenic wonders includes white-sand beaches, emerald-green rain forests, towering volcanoes, and rushing rivers.

Colombia is also home to many vibrant cities. Bogotá, the capital, is one of South America's great cities. As the nation's political, financial, and cultural heart, Bogotá has sometimes been called the Athens of South America because it has so many libraries and universities. The beautiful city of Cartagena lies on the Caribbean coast. The city, filled with cobblestone streets and handsome buildings, is alive with music.

Yet Colombia also has a troubled history. Since the 1960s, violent rebel groups have operated in Colombia. Some young people join rebel armies to escape poverty.

Opposite: **People fill the narrow streets of Cartagena. Founded in 1533, it is one of the oldest colonial cities in Colombia.**

COLOMBIA

- ● Cities of more than 500,000 people
- ○ Other cities
- ✪ National capital

0　　　　　　　　200 miles

0　　　　　200 kilometers

Caribbean Sea

Tayrona Nat'l Park
Riohacha
Santa Marta　Maicao
Barranquilla
Aracataca
Sabanalarga
Cartagena
Arjona
Carmen
Valledupar
Sierra Nevada de Santa Marta Nat'l Park
Sincelejo
Magangué
Catatumbo Barí Nat'l Park
Lorica
Montería
El Banco
Turbo
Ocaña
Caucasia
Cúcuta
Paramillo Nat'l Park
Pamplona
Barrancabermeja
Toma Nat'l Park
Bucaramanga
Arauca
Medellín
El Cocuy Nat'l Park
Sonsón
Nuquí
Quibdó
Sogamoso
Tunja
Aquitania
Puerto Carreño
Manizales
Armero
Zipaquirá
Yopal
El Tuparro Nat'l Park
Pereira
Chingaza Nat'l Park
Armenia
Bogotá
Buenaventura
Buga
Ibagué
Villavicencio
Las Hermosas Nat'l Park
Cali
Sumapaz Nat'l Park
Puerto Inírida
Palmira
Farallones de Cali Nat'l Park
Sierra de la Macarena Nat'l Park
Tierradentro
Neiva
El Charco
Popayán
Cordillera de los Picachos Nat'l Park
San José del Guaviare
Puracé Nat'l Park
Garzón
Tinigua Nat'l Park
Calamar
Tumaco
San Agustín
Pasto
Mocoa
Florencia
San Felipe
Ipiales
Mitú
Chiribiquete Nat'l Park
La Poya Nat'l Park
La Tagua
Araracuara
La Pedrera
Cahuinarí Nat'l Park
El Encanto
Río Puré Nat'l Park
Putumayo R.
Amacayacu Nat'l Park
Leticia

PANAMA

PACIFIC OCEAN

VENEZUELA

Magdalena R.

Meta R.

Orinoco R.

Guaviare R.

Caquetá R.

Amazon R.

ECUADOR

PERU

BRAZIL

Colombia

Others are forced to join against their will. Thousands of people have been killed in the fights between the rebels and those who oppose them. Millions more have fled their homes to seek safety from the violence.

During this time, Colombia became the world's leading producer and distributor of the illegal drug cocaine. Cocaine is made from the coca plant, which grows mainly in the Andes Mountains in nearby Bolivia and Peru, although the plant also grows in Colombia. The leaf of the coca plant is a mild stimulant, which Andean peoples have used for thousands of years. The leaf is also a source of flavoring, most famously for Coca-Cola. The leaf becomes cocaine only after it is chemically processed. Countless tons of coca leaves are processed into cocaine in Colombia each year. The cocaine is then shipped around the world.

A man harvests coca leaves in the mountains of Colombia.

Colombian Names

Colombians, like many Spanish-speaking people, often have two last names. The first last name comes from the father's family, and the second last name comes from the mother's family. The president of Colombia (right) is named Juan Manuel Santos Calderón. "Santos" comes from his father's family and "Calderón" from his mother's. Sometimes people use both last names; other times they use only the name from the father. The current president is usually called Juan Manuel Santos.

There is a vast fortune to be made from the cocaine trade. For this reason, many criminal organizations have gotten involved in its production and sale. For decades, rebels, drug dealers, and illegal armies called paramilitaries have waged a bloody war to control the cocaine industry. Innocent citizens frequently suffer from the violence, and many live in constant fear for their lives.

Colombia's leaders, however, have not ignored their nation's problems. In recent years, significant progress has been made to curb the rebel groups and drug dealers. In 2013, government peace negotiators under the direction of Colombian president Juan Manuel Santos worked to settle important differences with the Revolutionary Armed Forces of Colombia (FARC), the largest rebel group in the country. The negotiations provide hope to Colombians, who have grown weary with the country's ongoing problems.

Colombia is a close ally of the United States. In part because of that alliance, the government has adopted tough antidrug policies. In 2012, farmers grew 118,000 acres (47,750 hectares) of coca, a huge decline from the year 2000 when farmers cultivated 402,000 acres (162,700 ha). Annual cocaine production has plummeted from 772 tons (700 metric tons) in 2001 to 220 tons (200 metric tons) in 2012.

Colombia's potential for growth is unique among Latin American countries. It has excellent ports on both its Atlantic and Pacific coasts. Colombians are well educated, with a 90 percent literacy rate among adults. The country has a broad-based economy. As crime in the nation has plummeted in recent years, tourism has jumped dramatically. From 2003 to 2013, tourism increased 300 percent. No one can predict what the future holds for Colombia, but to many, the years ahead look bright.

A carriage driver shows tourists around Cartagena. About three million foreign visitors travel to Colombia every year.

CHAPTER 2

Natural Wonders

THE REPUBLIC OF COLOMBIA LIES IN THE NORTH-western corner of South America. It covers 439,736 square miles (1,138,911 square kilometers), about twice the size of the state of Texas. Colombia is South America's fourth-largest country, after Brazil, Argentina, and Peru. It was named after the explorer Christopher Columbus.

Colombia shares borders with Venezuela to the northeast, Brazil to the east and southeast, Peru to the south, and Ecuador to the southwest. In the northwest, Colombia borders the Central American nation of Panama. The Isthmus of Panama is a narrow strip of land that connects Central and South America. Colombia also borders on two major bodies of water: the Pacific Ocean in the west and the Caribbean Sea in the north.

Colombia has four major geographic zones. They are the Andes Mountains; the Caribbean and Pacific lowlands; the eastern Llanos plains; and the Amazon region in the south.

Opposite: **Tayrona National Park, on the Caribbean Sea, features massive boulders along a spectacular beach.**

Colombia's Geographic Features

Highest Elevation: Cristóbal Colón, 18,946 feet (5,775 m) above sea level

Lowest Elevation: Sea level, along the coasts

Longest River: Magdalena River (below), 968 miles (1,558 km)

Largest Lake: Lake Tota, 21 square miles (54 sq km)

Largest City (2011 est.): Bogotá, population 7,571,345

Area: 439,736 square miles (1,138,911 sq km)

Average High Temperature: In January, 68°F (20°C) in Bogotá, 90°F (32°C) in Cali; in July, 66°F (19°C) in Bogotá, 91°F (33°C) in Cali

Average Low Temperature: In January, 46°F (8°C) in Bogotá, 62°F (17°C) in Cali; in July, 49°F (9°C) in Bogotá, 60°F (15°C) in Cali

Average Annual Rainfall: 118 inches (300 cm)

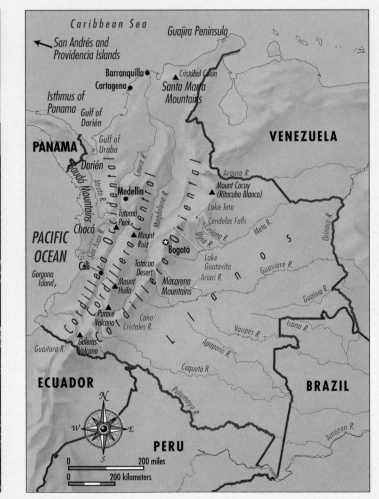

The Andes Mountains

The Andes Mountains stretch roughly 5,500 miles (8,900 kilometers), extending the length of South America. They run from the southern tip of the continent to the northern-most coast of Venezuela. In Colombia, the Andes occupy the entire length of the country's west coast.

Three mountain ranges, or *cordilleras*, make up the Andes Mountains in Colombia. These three cordilleras cover about one-third of Colombia's total land area.

The Cordillera Oriental is the most easterly and the largest of Colombia's mountain ranges. The Cordillera Oriental curves sharply to the northwest as it nears Colombia's border with Venezuela. The highest point in the range is Ritacuba Blanco, at 17,749 feet (5,410 meters). It rises among the snowcapped peaks of El Cocuy National Park, in the north. The capital

Colombia's towering mountains frequently reach into the clouds.

A small lake sits amid the rocky heights of El Cocuy National Park.

city of Bogotá stands on a high plateau in the middle of the Cordillera Oriental, at 8,612 feet (2,625 m) above sea level.

The Santa Marta range, a detached section of the Cordillera Oriental, lies on the Caribbean coast. It includes Colombia's highest point, Cristóbal Colón (Spanish for Christopher Columbus), which reaches 18,946 feet (5,775 m) above sea level. On the northern side of the Santa Marta range is the Guajira Peninsula. This desert region is split between Colombia and Venezuela.

The Cordillera Central lies next to the Cordillera Oriental and begins at Colombia's border with Ecuador. This range includes several volcanoes, including the 14,028-foot (4,276 m) Galeras, which last erupted in 2010. The highest peak in the Cordillera Central is the volcano Mount Huila, which rises to 18,865 feet (5,750 m). The second-highest peak is the volcanic Mount Ruiz, at 17,425 feet (5,311 m). In 1985, it erupted, melting about 10 percent of its ice cap. The melting caused a mudflow that carried millions of tons of slush and volcanic material over the town of Armero and a nearby village. More than twenty-five thousand people were killed in this natural disaster, the deadliest in Colombia's history.

The Cordillera Occidental runs parallel to the Pacific Ocean north from the Ecuadorian border. It is the lowest of the three cordilleras and does not have year-round snow. Its highest point is Tatamá, at 13,940 feet (4,250 m). The city of Cali, sitting 3,280 feet (1,000 m) above sea level, lies just to the east of the range.

A cloud of ash and steam erupts from Mount Huila. It is the highest volcano in Colombia.

The Tumaco Earthquake

On December 12, 1979, a powerful earthquake rocked the area near the border between Colombia and Ecuador. The earthquake triggered a tsunami, a series of huge ocean waves, which destroyed six fishing villages and killed roughly six hundred people. Another four thousand people were injured. All the homes in the town of Charco were seriously damaged or destroyed.

There, powerful tsunami waves washed the houses into a nearby lake. In Tumaco, 50 miles (80 km) from the earthquake's center, about one-tenth of all the buildings were destroyed, including 1,280 houses. The damage caused by the earthquake led to the adoption of a national building code in 1984, which called for buildings to be able to resist earthquake damage.

The Caribbean Lowlands

A man makes his way through swampy waters in the Caribbean Lowlands.

The Caribbean Lowlands cover northern Colombia, from the border with Panama to the Guajira Peninsula in the east. The lowlands form roughly a triangular shape, with the longest side

being the Caribbean coast. Swamps, streams, and small lakes dot the region, which features many banana and cotton plantations. A lush rain forest in the Darién region near Panama has one of the highest levels of plant and animal diversity in the world.

The Chocó region is filled with lush rain forests. More than eight thousand different species of plants grow in the area.

The Pacific Lowlands

The Pacific Lowlands lie between the Pacific Ocean and the Cordillera Occidental. The northern part of this region is called the Chocó. In the northeast, the Pacific Lowlands reach all the way to the Gulf of Darién, the southern part of the Caribbean Sea that lies east of Panama and north of Colombia. From there, the lowlands stretch for roughly 500 miles (800 km) southward along the Pacific coast. This narrow coastal region is filled with lagoons, thick rain forests, and salty swamplands.

The rain forests of the Pacific Lowlands are home to abundant mammals, birds, butterflies, insects, reptiles, and amphibians. An average of 354 inches (899 centimeters) of rain falls at Quibdó, the capital of this region, every year, making the Chocó one of the wettest places on Earth. The heavy rains produce fast-moving rapids in the rivers that flow from the Cordillera Occidental to the Pacific Ocean.

But the largest river in the Chocó, the Atrato, does not flow into the Pacific. Instead it flows northward, emptying into the Gulf of Urabá, a narrow inlet at the southern end of the Gulf of Darién. The Atrato Valley separates the Baudó Mountains from the Cordillera Occidental. These lower mountains, which rise to about 5,900 feet (1,800 m) near the Isthmus of Panama, are covered with dense forests.

The Llanos

The Llanos are vast, flat plains that stretch across the northern part of eastern Colombia. The llanos cover an area of 220,000 square miles (570,000 sq km)—about 70 percent of the land in Colombia—but they are home to less than 3 percent of the nation's total population. A small branch of the Andes called the Macarena Mountains rises in the western part of the Llanos.

Many rivers cross the Llanos, including the Orinoco, one of South America's largest rivers, which forms part of the border between Colombia and Venezuela. Today, the Llanos are Colombia's main oil-producing region. Cattle raising is also an important economic activity in this area.

The southern portion of eastern Colombia includes part of the mighty Amazon River. In total, the river runs for roughly 4,300 miles (6,900 km), making it the world's second-longest river, after the Nile in Africa. The Amazon River accounts for about 50 miles (80 km) of Colombia's border with Peru. Many rivers that flow into the Amazon begin in the Cordillera Oriental. Tropical rain forest covers most of Colombia's Amazonian region. Few people live in the area. The indigenous people who live in the Amazon are skilled at making medicine from rain forest plants.

Rivers and Lakes

The Magdalena River, which flows in between the Cordillera Central and the Cordillera Oriental, is the longest river in Colombia. It rises in southwestern Colombia and runs for 968 miles (1,558 km) before reaching the Caribbean Sea. The Magdalena's river basin—the area that drains into the

Vast plains cover much of southern Colombia.

Magdalena—covers about 24 percent of Colombia. Four of the country's largest cities—Bogotá, Medellín, Cali, and Barranquilla—are located in the Magdalena's river basin, and roughly 75 percent of the country's population lives in this region. Since before Europeans arrived in South America, the Magdalena has served as a vital route for moving people and goods from the interior of South America to coastal regions.

The Cauca River lies between the Cordillera Occidental and the Cordillera Central. It rises near Popayán in southwestern Colombia and runs for 838 miles (1,350 km) before it joins the Magdalena River in Magangué. Industrial waste produced in Popayán and by gold mines and coal mines in the countryside have polluted the river. In some places, the pollution is so bad that the river is unable to support plant or animal life.

Several large rivers in eastern Colombia provide the main mode of transportation in that region. The Ariari and

The Liquid Rainbow

Caño Cristales is a river located in the Cordillera Oriental. It is commonly called the "River of Five Colors" or the "Liquid Rainbow" because of its dazzling green, yellow, blue, red, and black hues. For most of the year, Caño Cristales looks like any other river. But for a few weeks from September to November, a species of plant that grows on the river floor turns a brilliant red. Patches of yellow and green sand, blue water, and dozens of others shades add to the vibrant explosion of color. The Liquid Rainbow, which flows within Sierra de la Macarena National Park, is a popular tourist attraction.

A colorful bridge connects Providencia and Santa Catalina Islands in the Caribbean Sea.

Guaviare Rivers separate the Llanos in the north from the Amazon region in the south. The Guaviare and rivers to its north, including the Meta and Arauca, drain into the Orinoco River. The rivers south of the Guaviare, including the Vaupés, Caquetá, and Putumayo, flow into the Amazon.

Lake Tota is the largest lake in Colombia, with a surface area of 21 square miles (54 sq km). It is located just north of Bogotá. Lake Tota is the source of the Upía River, which flows eastward into the basin of the Orinoco River. Aquitania is the largest town on the lake, lying on the eastern shore.

Islands

Many islands are part of Colombia. The largest are San Andrés and Providencia, which are part of a chain of islands in the Caribbean Sea about 470 miles (760 km) northwest of Barranquilla. In the seventeenth century, English pirates attacking Spanish ships used the islands as a base of operations.

The blue anole lives only on Gorgona Island. Both the male and female of the species are blue.

The smaller Rosario Islands, near the city of Cartagena on the Caribbean coast, are a national park. The park was established to protect one of the coastline's coral reefs and the plants and sea life that live there.

Most of the Pacific coast islands are small and not far from the shore of Colombia. Gorgona Island lies about 22 miles (35 km) off the coast. Once used as a prison, today it is a national park that protects many unusual species such as the blue anole, a type of lizard that is entirely blue.

Malpelo Island is a small island located 310 miles (500 km) off the port of Buenaventura. Except for a Colombian military outpost, the island is uninhabited. A small nature reserve is home to protected plant and wildlife species. Malpelo is a popular shark diving destination. Visitors come to see the large populations of hammerhead and silky sharks that swim in the waters near the island.

Climate

Colombia's climate has a broad range of temperatures, due mainly to differences in elevation. Temperatures are very hot at sea level and get cooler as elevations get higher.

The country is divided into three climatic zones. Elevations below 3,000 feet (900 m) are known as *tierra caliente*, or the "hot zone." Annual average temperatures there run between 75 degrees Fahrenheit (24 degrees Celsius) and 81°F (27°C). About 86 percent of Colombia's total area lies in the hot zone.

Elevations of 3,000 to 6,500 feet (900 to 2,000 m) are the *tierra templada*, or the "temperate zone." Temperatures there

Camera operators try to protect their equipment during a downpour in Barranquilla, along the Caribbean coast. This area is hot and humid, and rainfall is common between May and November.

Animals graze on the meager grasses of the Guajira Peninsula.

are often between 65°F and 75°F (18°C and 24°C). Above this lies the *tierra fría*, the "cold zone." This includes cities such as Bogotá, which has an annual average temperature of 57°F (14°C). The temperate and cold zones together make up 14 percent of the country's land, but the majority of the people in Colombia live there.

In the highest mountain reaches, above 10,000 feet (3,000 m), frigid temperatures of 1.5°F to 9°F (–17°C to –13°C) are common. Many of Colombia's peaks above 15,000 feet (4,600 m) are covered with ice and snow year-round.

Rainfall is heaviest in the Pacific Lowlands and in the Amazon forests in eastern Colombia. In some parts of the lowlands, rainfall can reach 300 inches (760 cm) annually. Some regions of the Chocó receive as much as 400 inches (1,000 cm) per year. The Guajira Peninsula is the driest place in Colombia. It receives an annual rainfall of about only 10 inches (25 cm).

Looking at Colombia's Cities

The capital of Bogotá is Colombia's largest city, home to 7,571,345 people in 2011. Medellín (right), which is home to 3,729,970 people, is Colombia's second-largest city. The metropolitan section of Medellín lies in a valley at an elevation of about 4,900 feet (1,500 m). The Medellín River runs through the city. Medellín is a center for coffee, food processing, and fashion. The city has an efficient mass transit system that includes hanging gondola cars, which carry people up the steep hillsides. Popular attractions include the Arví Ecotourism Park, the Metropolitan Theater, and the Museum of Modern Art.

Cali is Colombia's third-largest city, with a population of 3,225,580. Explorer Sebastían de Belalcázar founded Cali in 1536. The city lies about 3,300 feet (1,000 m) above sea level on fairly flat ground. It is the center for Colombia's sugar industry. Cali is also a popular tourist destination, with such highlights as the Ermita Church (left) and La Plaza de Toros de Cañaveralejo, the largest bullring in Colombia. The city is well known for salsa music, which is featured in Cali's many nightclubs and dance venues.

Barranquilla is Colombia's fourth-largest city, with a population of 2,185,359. Founded in 1629, it is now the country's main Caribbean seaport and a center of the textile industry. Barranquilla is hot year-round, often with high levels of humidity. The city is famous for its annual carnival in February.

CHAPTER 3

Magnificent Wildlife

FEW PLACES ON EARTH CAN RIVAL COLOMBIA'S amazing variety of plant and animal life. Although Colombia covers only 1 percent of the planet's surface, it is home to 14 percent of the world's known species. The nation is home to thirty-five thousand plant species, more than six hundred amphibian species, and 475 species of reptile. About 450 species of mammals live in Colombia, as well as 1,800 species of birds. This accounts for almost 20 percent of all the bird species in the world. One-third of the country's plant species and 12 percent of its animal species are endemic, meaning they live in Colombia and nowhere else.

Opposite: **Four species of sloths live in Colombia. These gentle animals spend almost all their time hanging in trees.**

In the Páramos

Regions called *páramos* lie in the highest reaches of the Andes Mountains. The páramos are blanketed in continuous rain, fog, and misty clouds. Small lakes, swamps, and ravines dot the landscape. Though generally cold and humid, páramos often experience sudden changes in temperature. Temperatures can vary from below freezing to highs of 86°F (30 °C).

Frailejones thrive in cold, dry regions high in the mountains.

Short trees, such as the mortiño and the pagoda, have adapted to survive the extreme conditions at these high elevations. Mosses, grasses, and hardy shrubs grow well in marshy areas. Several species of shrubs called *frailejones* (tall friars) grow in the páramos. The trunks of these unique shrubs are thick and have fuzz-covered leaves that protect against the cold. The frailejones flowers are yellow, and look like daisies.

Wildlife in the páramos includes Andean foxes, guinea pigs, rat opossums, and white-tailed deer. Birds that frequent the páramos include Andean condors, turkey buzzards, hawks, and falcons. Insects such as grasshoppers and beetles and mollusks such as snails and slugs are also found in the páramos. One of the most unusual creatures found in the páramos is an earthworm that grows to almost 5 feet (1.5 m) long.

Andean Highlands

The lower slopes of the Andes are a mix of wet forests and open grasslands. As the human population has grown through the centuries, the area that has been cleared for agriculture has grown. The Colombian government is trying to preserve what remains of the country's diverse wildlife and delicate ecosystems. Today, fifty-six national parks, preserves, and sanctuaries are spread throughout the country. Many of them are located in the mountains.

Chingaza National Park is located in the Cordillera Oriental. It is estimated that more than two thousand different species of plants can be found in the park. The park is home to many types of birds, including Andean condors,

The High-Soaring Condor

Colombia's national bird is the Andean condor. A magnificent vulture with a wingspan of 11 feet (3 m), it is one of the world's largest and heaviest birds. Males can weigh as much as 33 pounds (15 kilograms) and females 24 pounds (11 kg). A remarkable flier, the condor can travel more than 600 miles (1,000 km) in a single day. The Andean condor is said to symbolize the Colombian people's freedom and strength.

Since the early 1970s, the Andean condor has been an endangered species. Human activity and land development threatened the condor's natural habitat. These birds could no longer find the food they eat. The number of Andean condors dwindled significantly. By the mid-1980s, only about 15 condors lived in Colombia.

To stem the species' decline, many zoos and nature preserves raise condors in captivity and then release them into the wild. Thanks to their efforts, the population of the Andean condor in Colombia is growing steadily. Today, there are about 150 of these splendid birds soaring over the Andes.

turkeys, and toucans. Spectacled bear, deer, monkeys, and jaguars roam the lower reaches of the park.

Las Hermosas National Park is located in the highest elevations of the Cordillera Central. The Magdalena and the Cauca Rivers border the park. Las Hermosas's 387 lakes are home to a wide variety of algae that provide food to many kinds of fish, including trout. Plants that grow in the cold rain forests include encenillo trees, which contain chemicals that are used to cure leather and color it red. A type of alder tree is the main plant that grows along streams. The park is home to a wide variety of birds, including the scaly-naped parrot, the band-tailed pigeon, the red-backed hawk, and several species

The keel-billed toucan lives in rain forests from southern Mexico to northern South America. Because it sports many bright colors, it is sometimes known as the rainbow toucan.

A Visit to Puracé National Natural Park

Puracé National Natural Park is located southeast of the city of Popayán in the Cordillera Central range. The Colombian government established it as a national park in 1961. It features deep canyons, bubbling hot springs, and roaring waterfalls. But the park's main attraction is Puracé, the 15,256-foot (4,650 m) active volcano, which last erupted in 1977.

Puracé National Natural Park is home to more than two hundred species of orchids along with endangered trees such as the Colombian pine, the Andean oak, and the wax palm, Colombia's national tree. Among the 150 species of birds found in the park are the Andean condor and the black-and-chestnut eagle. The lower reaches of the forest are home to four monkey species: the woolly monkey, the red howler monkey (below), the

brown capuchin, and the lemurine owl monkey. Mice, bats, weasels, bears, and pumas also make the forest their homes. The world's smallest species of deer, the northern pudu, which stands scarcely more than 12 inches (30 cm) at the shoulder, survives there as well.

Several indigenous, or native, groups of people live in the park. The Páez people live near the Puracé volcano. Their ancestors were driven off their original homelands on the western slope of the central mountain range by the Spaniards. They resettled in the forests that make up the park today. The Yanacona people also live in the park, in the foothills of the Sotará volcano.

Tourists can stay at camping areas or in cabins within the park. Many visitors also plan trips to nearby San Juan hot springs and the San Nicolás waterfall.

of hummingbirds. Pumas, weasels, rabbits, and small tailless rodents called cavies are also found in the park.

Most regions in the Colombian Andes are green and colorful with plant life, but a few areas are desertlike. The Tatacoa Desert, in the upper Magdalena River valley, is an area of dry canyons and weathered rock. Cactuses and hardy shrubs are the only plants that can survive the high temperatures and lack of rainfall. Rodents, spiders, snakes, and eagles live in the desert.

The Santa Marta Mountains

One of the most biologically diverse regions in Colombia is the Santa Marta range. This isolated mountain range is home to several ecosystems, including tropical rain forests, shrubland, and páramos.

The rain forest is thick with trees that often grow as tall as 130 feet (40 m). More than three thousand species of plants

A Deadly Frog

A poison dart frog called the red-banded poison frog, or Lehmann's frog, lives in the rain forests of Colombia. Its beautiful body features brightly colored patterns of red, orange, or yellow with a black or dark brown background. The frogs live near water, although some thrive in small bushes and trees. The frog's colorful pattern warns its enemies that it is poisonous. Indigenous peoples once used the frog's poison on the tip of blowgun darts when they hunted. Researchers have found that the frog does not make its own poison. It uses the chemicals from the food it eats, such as ants and mites, to make the poison.

live in the Santa Marta Mountains. Some plants, such as moss and ferns, grow on the trees. Long-stemmed, woody vines also grow up the trees. The vines use the trees as support to climb to the top of the forest in order to reach sunlight.

Many brightly colored birds live in these mountains, including parakeets, warblers, hummingbirds, and trogons. About 630 species of birds have been recorded in the small area. That's roughly one-third of all bird species found in the country. Other animals that live in the range include jaguars, brocket deer, cougars, armadillos, and anteaters. One of the most unusual creatures found here is the tapir. This large mammal is shaped like a pig but is related to the horse and the rhinoceros.

Tayrona National Park, on the northern edge of the range, protects about 108 species of mammals and three hundred species of birds. More than seventy species of bats also reside there. The park's wide, sandy beaches are nesting sites for green sea turtles.

A Spectacular Orchid

Colombia's national flower is the orchid *Cattleya trianae*, sometimes called the *flor de Mayo*, or May flower. It is named after an English botanist named William Cattley and a Colombian botanist named José Jerónimo Triana. The lip of the flower is yellow, blue, and red—the same colors as the flag of Colombia. The delicate orchid grows high up in forests, at altitudes of 5,000 to 6,500 feet (1,500 to 2,000 m). Today, the *Cattleya trianae* is an endangered species in Colombia because so much of its habitat has been destroyed.

Rain Forests

Colombia's abundant and lush rain forests are home to an incredible variety of life. Birds such as toucans and macaws are found in many areas. Spider monkeys, sloths, howler monkeys, and capuchins live in the trees of the forest. They feed upon seeds, leaves, and fruits. Animals such as mice, paca, poison dart frogs, and giant anteaters roam the forest floor.

Many species thrive in and around the rivers in the rain forest. The capybara, the largest rodent on Earth, lives along the banks of the Amazon and its tributaries. An excellent swimmer, it grows to about 4 feet (1.2 m) long and can weigh 100 pounds (45 kg). The giant river otter, the world's largest otter, feeds on small reptiles and fish. Electric eels and giant catfish are commonly found in the rain forests. Amazonian manatees thrive in the Amazonian river system. They are wrinkled, almost hairless water mammals that can reach 9 feet (3 m) long and weigh up to 1,200 pounds (540 kg). Birds such as storks, egrets, and herons live along lagoons and shallow pools of water.

The Llanos

The Llanos plains cover much of Colombia. The land is covered by a mixture of dry grasslands and forests. Many rivers cut through these grasslands, causing floods in parts of the Llanos during the rainy season. This makes it a magnificent wetland region that supports abundant wildlife. More than seven hundred species of birds have been seen there. This is as many as are in the entire United States. These include waterbirds such as scarlet ibises, sandpipers, and yellowlegs. The Llanos also shelter endangered species such as the giant armadillo and the Orinoco turtle. The world's most endangered reptile also lives in the Llanos. The Orinoco crocodile grows up to about 17 feet (5 m) long. It was widely hunted in the nineteenth and twentieth centuries, and today fewer than 1,500 of these creatures survive.

The giant armadillo is covered by a flexible shell made of horn and bone. When threatened, the armadillo sometimes rolls up into a ball.

CHAPTER 4

Conquest and Independence

ISTORIANS BELIEVE THAT THE EARLIEST HUMAN settlements in the region that is now Colombia date to before 20,000 BCE. Some of the earliest people to settle in the region were in the Cordillera Central, the Cordillera Oriental, and the Cauca River valley. These early peoples were hunter-gatherers. They hunted, fished, and gathered nuts, fruits, and seeds to survive. By roughly 2000 BCE, they began to farm, growing corn, potatoes, yucca, and other crops.

Native Colombians

By 1500 CE, various native groups lived in what is now Colombia. The Tairona people lived in the north, along the Caribbean coast and in the Santa Marta Mountains. The Taironas constructed towns and built paved roads, large stone temples, and aqueducts for carrying water to fields. They also fished and traded with nearby groups.

The Muisca lived in the countryside near what is now Bogotá. They grew crops and used simple wooden tools.

The Statues of San Agustín

More than three hundred enormous stone statues dominate the landscape at an archaeological site near Popayán, high in the Andes. The figures represent gods and mythical animals. Some of the carvings are human figures that are smiling or frowning. Some of the stones show snakes, frogs, jaguars, or large birds. These mysterious sculptures guard burial sites. The oldest statues at San Agustín are believed to be two thousand years old. The site holds the largest collection of ancient monumental sculptures in South America.

Unlike the sturdy stone structures built by the Tairona people, the Muiscas' homes and temples were made of thatched wood. The Muiscas also traded gold, emeralds, and textiles. By the early sixteenth century, the Muiscas numbered roughly six hundred thousand and were the wealthiest and most powerful indigenous group in Colombia.

Another indigenous group, the Sinú people, lived southwest of the Taironas in the lower Magdalena River valley. The Tumaco people settled on the Pacific coast, and the Quimbayas farmed the lowlands in western Colombia. Other groups, such as the Tolimas and Calimas, lived in the central and southern highlands.

Skilled indigenous craftspeople produced handsome ceramic pottery and beautiful items of gold. They found the gold along the riverbeds and streams of the region's countless waterways. In some places, they mined the gold from mountains.

The Coming of the Europeans

The first Europeans to see present-day Colombia were Olonso de Ojeda and his crew, who sailed from Spain in 1499. Ojeda sailed along the Guajira Peninsula in search of gold. Expeditions by Rodrigo de Bastidas and Juan de la Cosa followed in the next two years. In 1525, Bastidas established the first Spanish settlement in what is now Colombia, at Santa Marta. In 1533, Spanish conqueror Pedro de Heredia founded Cartagena, which was to become an important trading port.

Soon, rumors of gold, gems, and other treasures convinced the Spaniards to explore farther inland. In 1536, Gonzalo Jiménez de Quesada led an expedition up the Magdalena River into the homeland of the Muiscas. After battling disease, swamp insects, and hunger—and losing more than half his men in a shipwreck—Quesada finally arrived at his destination in early 1537.

The indigenous people tried to defend their lands from Quesada and his men, but with superior weapons, the Europeans quickly ended the resistance. Quesada's forces destroyed indigenous villages and raided the royal capital of

European Exploration

→ Olonso de Ojeda, 1499–1502

→ Sebastián de Belalcázar, 1533–1539

→ Gonzalo Jiménez de Quesada, 1536–1537

→ Nikolaus Federmann, 1537–1539

Present-day border

The Mystery of El Dorado

When the Spaniards arrived in the land of the Muiscas, they heard tales of a strange ritual: the ceremony of El Dorado, or "The Golden One," which is depicted in the gold pieces shown right. According to an account written by a Spanish soldier, the ceremony took place on the day the Muiscas gained a new ruler. The new ruler was taken to Lake Guatavita where he made offerings to the Muisca gods. A raft was made of reeds and decorated with ornate objects. The new leader was stripped of all his clothes and covered completely with gold dust. Then the raft was loaded with piles of gold and emeralds. The man and four of his most important nobles, wearing crowns and bracelets of gold and fine clothing, set off upon the lake in the raft. When they reached the middle of the lake, the chief and his nobles tossed all the gold and emeralds into the water. Then the chief dived into the lake to wash the gold dust from his body.

Eager to gain possession of the valuable treasures, the Spaniards launched several unsuccessful expeditions to Lake Guatavita. They even tried draining the lake in the hopes of discovering the gold and emeralds at its bottom. To this day, no one has found the fabled riches that are supposed to be in the lake.

the Muisca people. Quesada was now in control of the entire Muisca territory. In 1538, he founded the city of Santa Fé de Bogotá, present-day Bogotá.

A statue of Sebastián de Belalcázar stands in Cali, a city he founded in 1536.

Meanwhile, two other expeditions were heading toward the newly conquered Muisca territory. Nikolaus Federmann, a German serving the Spanish crown, was coming from western Venezuela. Sebastián de Belalcázar led the second expedition from Quito, Ecuador. Belalcázar had served in Peru during the Spanish conquest of the Incas. On his journey toward Muisca territory, he founded the towns of Popayán and Cali in southern Colombia.

Rather than fight for control of the captured territory, the leaders of the three expeditions agreed to let authorities in Spain decide which European group would possess the land. In 1549, the Spanish crown created the Real Audiencia of

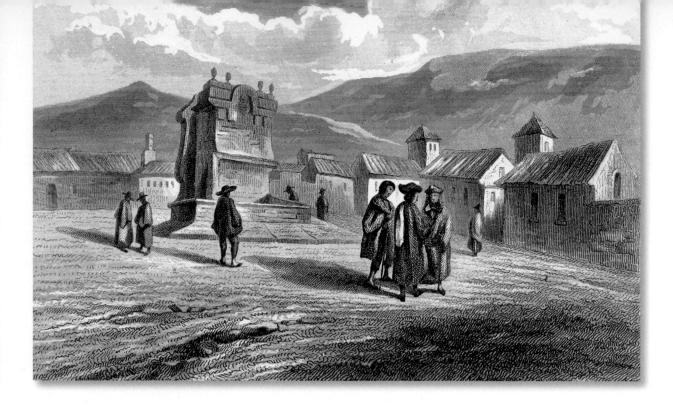

In the 1700s, Bogotá was the largest city in what is now Colombia. By 1789, about eighteen thousand people lived there.

Santa Fé de Bogotá. The *audiencia*, or court, would manage the affairs of Colombia. The audiencia was under the control of the Viceroyalty of Peru. The viceroyalty was a governing district that oversaw all Spanish settlements in South America and Panama.

Colonial Society

The lure of fertile land, gold, and emeralds brought a steady flow of new settlers to Spain's new colony. To provide the labor needed to work the fields and the mines, the Spanish government created the *encomienda* system. Settlers were "given" a number of indigenous people who would provide labor and pay tribute. The colonists were to protect the indigenous workers, convert them to Christianity, and teach them Spanish in return for this labor. In reality, there was little difference between the encomienda system and slavery. The indigenous people were forced to work and lost their land and freedom. Enslaved Africans were also brought to Colombia and forced to work as servants, gold miners, and plantation laborers.

Over time, as the Europeans, indigenous peoples, and Africans in Colombia lived and worked together, they began to have children together, too. The racial makeup of the new colony changed rapidly.

Rising Tensions

In 1717, Spain established a large colony called the Viceroyalty of New Granada. The viceroyalty included what are now Colombia, Venezuela, Panama, and Ecuador. Santa Fé de Bogotá, usually known simply as Bogotá, was its capital. The city became a major hub of trade and settlement in Spain's empire in the Americas.

But all was not well in New Granada. Colonists resented being ruled by the faraway Spanish crown. The colonists paid high taxes and were forbidden to trade with other countries. Spain took the colony's gold and other resources. Colonists born in Colombia were excluded from many government jobs. Meanwhile, indigenous people living in New Granada were concerned with keeping land grants they had received from the crown, and Africans in the colony were seeking ways to achieve freedom. Colonists, indigenous people, and slaves all used the Spanish court system to demand more rights and freedoms. When the Spanish failed to make reforms, many came to resent the colonial system.

A Walking Tour of Cartagena

Cartagena, a historic port city on the Caribbean coast, is one of Colombia's most beautiful cities. It was founded in 1533 by Spanish commander Pedro de Heredia. The town was named after Cartagena, Spain, where most of Heredia's sailors had lived. Indigenous people had inhabited the area as early as 4,000 BCE.

Cartagena's Old Town features a stunning assortment of colonial mansions, historic churches, and grand plazas. Thick walls built to protect the city from invaders surround Old Town. Visitors can enter the city at the Torre del Reloj, a yellow clock tower that stands above the main gate (below). Beyond the entrance is

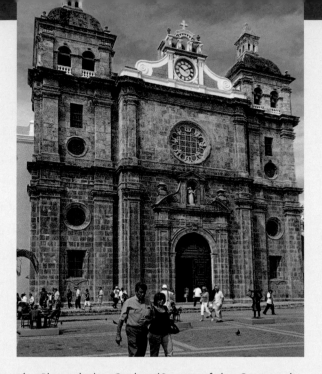

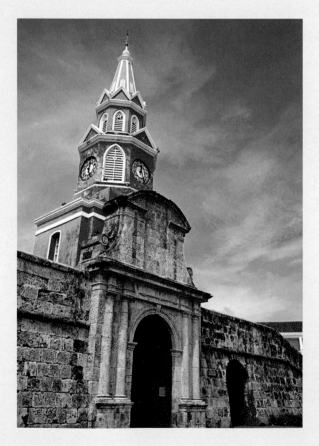

the Plaza de los Coches (Square of the Carriages), which was once a slave market where enslaved Africans were bought and sold.

Nearby is the Church of San Pedro Claver (above), built in 1580, and named for a priest who cared for the slaves. Not far are the Museum of Modern Art and the Naval Museum, two of the city's popular tourist destinations. The Palace of the Inquisition in Bolívar Plaza was where Catholic priests tortured people of other faiths in order to convert them to Catholicism. Now a museum, it houses an important collection of old maps of the New Kingdom of Granada. Close by is the Bartolomé Calvo Library, one of the country's largest public libraries, specializing in literature, history, and economics.

Outside the walls of Old Town stands the San Felipe de Barajas Castle, the strongest fort the Spaniards built in any of their colonies. A complex system of underground tunnels connects various parts of the fortress. Visitors can take tours of the tunnels and learn about the construction of this historic site.

Many settlers began to call for independence from Spain. The first uprising against Spanish rule occurred in 1781. The rebellion, known as the Comunero Revolt, spread to many parts of New Granada, but Spanish military forces eventually crushed it.

The Road to Independence

Chaotic events in Europe soon gave New Granada's colonists hope for independence. In 1808, French leader Napoleon Bonaparte overthrew the king of Spain, Ferdinand VII. During the upheaval, Spain paid little attention to its colonies. Rebels in several cities in New Granada seized the opportunity. They fought colonists who were loyal to Spain, and their cities broke away from the Spanish government. In 1810, the colonists of Cartagena set up an independent government. On July 20, 1810, Bogotá rose up in rebellion, an event now celebrated as Colombian Independence Day. In 1813, the Bogotá rebels formed the independent state of Cundinamarca.

In 1814, the Spanish king regained power after defeating the French. To reestablish authority in New Granada, the Spanish government sent troops to Colombia. Hundreds of rebel leaders were executed and the countryside was destroyed.

Rebel troops regrouped under General Francisco de Paula Santander. They joined forces with Simón Bolívar, a Venezuelan revolutionary leader spearheading the fight for independence. Bolívar recruited many Afro-Colombians to his army, promising them freedom if they fought for independence. *Llaneros*, cowboys from the Llanos, were also a vital part of Bolívar's army. On

August 7, 1819, the combined rebel forces defeated the Spanish at the Battle of Boyacá. Spain's rule of New Granada had ended.

On December 17, independence was declared with the founding of the Republic of Gran Colombia. The new state included Colombia, Ecuador, Venezuela, and Panama.

The New Nation

Simón Bolívar became the president of Gran Colombia, and General Francisco de Paula Santander was vice president. Bolívar was supported by the conservatives. Santander was supported by the liberals. The conservatives supported slavery, the Catholic Church, and a strong central government. The liberals favored a weaker central government and separation of church and state. Many liberals also opposed slavery. In 1821, Gran Colombia adopted its first constitution, which favored conservative beliefs.

Internal conflicts and the sheer size of Gran Colombia made it nearly impossible to govern. In 1830, Ecuador and Venezuela declared their independence. Civil wars erupted between the conservatives and liberals from 1839 to 1842. After the fighting, the government implemented new reforms that abolished

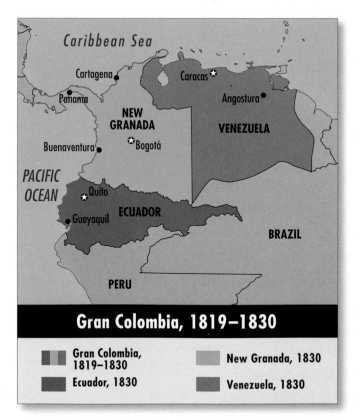

Gran Colombia, 1819–1830

Gran Colombia, 1819–1830
Ecuador, 1830
New Granada, 1830
Venezuela, 1830

The Rebel Spy

Policarpa Salavarrieta, also known as La Pola, was a dressmaker who spied for the rebel forces that fought for independence from Spain. Today she is considered a hero in Colombia's struggle for independence.

Few details exist about La Pola's early years. Her true name is unknown. At various times she went by the names Apolonia or Gregoria Apolinaria. Even her place of birth is clouded in mystery. Some say she was born in Guaduas or Mariquita, towns about 75 to 95 miles (120 to 150 km) from Bogotá, or even in the capital city itself.

By 1817, La Pola was living in Bogotá, where most of the population supported Spain and strongly opposed the rebels. It is believed she entered the city from Guaduas with forged documents. She stayed in the home of Andrea Ricaurte, a supporter of the resistance in the capital.

As a dressmaker and mender of clothing, La Pola was able to gain access to the homes of the wives and daughters of Spanish soldiers. She overheard conversations and gathered maps and other information about the army's plans. She also secretly encouraged young men to fight in the rebel cause.

Spanish authorities learned about La Pola's spying activities and searched for her throughout Bogotá. She was finally captured, and on November 14, 1817, she was executed by a firing squad.

Policarpa Salavarrieta is a national hero in Colombia. Her image has been used many times on Colombian money. Today, November 14 is known as the Day of the Colombian Woman, in honor of her death.

Barranquilla is located where the Magdalena River enters the Caribbean Sea. The city became an important port in the nineteenth century.

slavery, allowed for freedom of the press, and lowered taxes on imported goods. An amended constitution weakened the central government and passed power to regional governments.

In 1863, government officials rewrote Gran Colombia's constitution, and the country was renamed the United States of Colombia. The constitution created nine states that were granted strong powers of self-government. The states, however, continually disagreed with one another over trade issues and borders.

A new constitution in 1886 established the Republic of Colombia. Under it, the semi-independent states now came under tighter control of Bogotá.

Tensions between the conservatives and liberals increased throughout the nineteenth century. In 1899, a liberal revolt resulted in the War of a Thousand Days, which lasted three years. By the war's end, the liberals had been defeated and roughly one hundred thousand people had been killed. The war devastated the country's economy and weakened the government.

Amid the chaos of war, Panama declared its independence from the Republic of Colombia. The United States wanted to build a canal across the Isthmus of Panama, connecting the Atlantic and Pacific Oceans. When Colombia refused to go along with the plan, the United States threw its support behind Panamanian independence. The United States would help Panama separate from Colombia in exchange for the right to build the canal. This soured relations between Colombia and the United States for many years.

Workers harvest coffee on a plantation in Colombia.

As president, Enrique Olaya Herrera supported public education and the search for oil and other natural resources.

La Violencia

The conservatives held power until 1930. Under their leadership, Colombia's economy grew. The coffee and banana industries prospered, and oil was discovered along the Caribbean coast. New networks of roads and railroads were built, and a textile industry began to develop rapidly.

The liberals came to power with the election of Enrique Olaya Herrera in 1930, and they held power for the next sixteen years. Under their leadership, poor Colombians gained more civil rights. The economy grew, and laborers successfully pushed for better wages.

After the election of conservative Mariano Ospina Pérez in 1946, violence again erupted. In 1948, liberal leader Jorge Eliécer Gaitán was assassinated. His killing sparked violence in Bogotá, which spread to the countryside. Thousands of rural Colombians fled to cities to escape the devastation. This period became known as *La Violencia* (The Violence). It lasted from 1948 to 1962. An estimated two hundred thousand people were killed in this bloody conflict.

A New Partnership

In 1953, General Gustavo Rojas Pinilla overthrew the brutal conservative president Laureano Gómez. At first, Colombians supported Rojas, but he soon proved himself a corrupt dictator and lost the support of the country. The army overthrew him in 1957.

Liberals and conservatives then joined together to help bring peace to the divided nation. In 1958, the two parties created the National Front. This agreement stated that the parties would alternate in the presidency every four years until 1974. The legislature and other government and cabinet positions would be divided equally as well.

During the 1948 riots in Bogotá, streetcars were overturned and buildings were destroyed.

FARC troops guard a road in southwestern Colombia. At its height, FARC was estimated to have about eighteen thousand forces.

The National Front was a moderate success and brought Colombia a degree of political stability and economic growth. However, many felt excluded by the agreements made by the liberals and conservatives, and rebel groups began to form.

Rebel Fighters

Several rebel groups battled the government for control of the country's rural regions. These rebel groups wanted greater economic equality within Colombia. They also wanted to limit the influence of foreign nations and corporations. The Revolutionary Armed Forces of Colombia (or FARC, based on its initials in Spanish) and the National Liberation Army (ELN) emerged in the 1960s. The April 19 Movement, or M-19, formed in the early 1970s.

Both liberal and conservative administrations battled the rebels to drive them out of the many rural towns and villages they controlled. In an effort to end the fighting, conservative president Belisario Betancur proposed a cease-fire in 1982. The peace lasted only until 1985, when some groups resumed the warfare, more violently than ever before.

The Drug Trade

The business of selling illegal drugs also contributed to the chaos and violence in Colombia in the late twentieth century. Drug cartels are large business organizations that sell illegal drugs in order to make money. Beginning in the 1960s, Colombian drug cartels made huge sums of money producing

A police officer guards packages of marijuana seized in Cúcuta, in northeastern Colombia.

and selling marijuana and cocaine. Great quantities of the drugs were shipped to the United States.

In the 1980s, the cartel's armies killed many Colombian officials who opposed them, including policemen, judges, and politicians. In 1985, eleven Supreme Court judges were killed during a standoff at the Palace of Justice. President Virgilio Barco began waging war against the cartels in the late 1980s, resulting in an increase in drug-related violence. Bombings, assassinations, and kidnappings tore apart the country. During the 1990 presidential election, drug groups murdered three candidates.

During this time, many paramilitary groups arose. Some were backed by drug cartels, and others by wealthy business-people or political groups. They were dedicated to protecting their own interests. While many claimed to be fighting the

Colombian president Virgilio Barco (seated, second from left) and U.S. president George H. W. Bush (seated, second from right) joined other leaders at a conference on fighting the drug trade in 1990.

rebel groups, they often terrorized ordinary people. It is estimated that they killed tens of thousands of people.

In 2008, thousands of protesters filled Bogotá's main square, demanding that FARC release hostages they had kidnapped. FARC's influence has declined in recent years.

Plan Colombia

In 1999, President Andrés Pastrana Arango introduced Plan Colombia to end the armed conflict with rebels and drug dealers and shut down the drug trade. The United States contributed more than $3 billion in aid and hundreds of military and civilian personnel to assist the Colombian government.

Plan Colombia began to show signs of success during the administration of Álvaro Uribe Vélez, who was elected president in 2002. Some rebel groups stopped fighting and others lost much of their power. By 2010, the production of cocaine in Colombia had been reduced by 60 percent. Drug-related violence had also dropped dramatically.

The devastating effects of the drug trade and fighting continue to haunt Colombia. The nation has an estimated four million internal refugees, people who fled their homes to

U.S. forces greet children in Colombia in 2012. Several hundred U.S. military personnel work in Colombia.

escape the violence. Even as the activity of the paramilitaries, rebel groups, and drug cartels diminishes, the Colombian people continue to suffer.

Recent Years

Colombia's recent history has been marked by a series of disagreements with neighboring countries. In 2008, Colombian forces raided a rebel camp in Ecuador that they believed was being supported by the Ecuadorian government. Ecuador and Venezuela immediately sent forces to their borders. Colombian officials said that computer files seized in the raid supported their claim, but they apologized for entering Ecuadorian territory.

Tensions increased again in mid-2009 among the three nations over an agreement between the United States and Colombia. The agreement allowed U.S. troops to set up bases in Colombia to fight the drug trade. Venezuela and Ecuador, however, objected to American forces being so near.

Colombia has frequently accused Venezuela of providing support to Colombian rebels by giving them weapons or allowing them to operate within Venezuela's borders. Diplomatic relations remained strained between the two nations until Juan Manuel Santos was elected president of Colombia in 2010. Santos, who won on a platform of making peace with rebel groups, helped restore relations with Venezuela.

In late 2012, Santos announced that the Colombian government would begin negotiations with FARC to end the ongoing hostilities. By mid-2013, both sides reported that significant progress had been made. Although no cease-fire was in effect, violence was at a minimum. This alone gave hope to Colombians that the bloody conflict might end.

Commuters rush through the metro station in Medellín. This city, along with many others in Colombia, has prospered in recent years.

CHAPTER 5

Governing the Republic

COLOMBIA IS A DEMOCRATIC REPUBLIC. THIS MEANS that political power rests with the Colombian people, who elect government officials to represent them. Colombia is governed under a constitution adopted in 1991. The current version of the constitution, called the Constitution of Rights, was adopted on July 5, 1991. It replaced the constitution that had been in effect since 1886. Colombia's constitution divides its government into three branches: executive, legislative, and judicial.

Executive Branch

The president is the head of the executive branch. The president must be more than thirty years old, a citizen of the country, and Colombian by birth. Colombians vote to elect a president every four years. If no candidate receives more than 50 percent of the vote, a runoff election is held between the two people with the most votes. Presidents are allowed to serve two terms in a row. As in the United States, the presidential candidate selects his or her running mate for the office of vice president.

The National Flag

Colombia's flag consists of three horizontal bands of color: yellow, blue, and red. The yellow stripe, which covers the top half of the flag, represents the wealth of the nation. The blue stripe stands for the Atlantic and Pacific Oceans on the nation's borders. The red stripe stands for the blood shed to gain independence. The current flag was adopted in 1861.

María Ángela Holguín became the Colombian minister of foreign affairs in 2010.

The president is the head of state and the commander in chief of the armed forces. He or she is responsible for establishing economic policies and signing treaties with foreign nations. The president is sworn to maintain law and order and

President Santos

Juan Manuel Santos was elected president of Colombia in 2010. Born in 1951 in Bogotá, he studied at the Naval School at Cartagena and served in the Colombian navy until 1971. After leaving the navy, he attended school in the United States at the University of Kansas, and then in England at the London School of Economics. He returned to the United States where he earned degrees in economics and law at Tufts University in Massachusetts.

Santos began his political career by serving as minister of trade during the presidency of César Gaviria, from 1991 to 1994. In 2005, Santos helped found the Social Party of National Unity. For decades, the only major political parties in Colombia were the conservative and liberal parties. Voters responded positively to having another party by electing twenty senators and thirty deputies to the Colombian Congress. Today, the Social Party of National Unity is the dominant political party in Colombia, winning 28 percent of all seats in Congress in the 2010 elections.

Santos has attempted to negotiate an end to the conflict with the FARC rebels that has plagued Colombia since the 1970s. His goal is to achieve a lasting cease-fire.

to make certain that all Colombians are free to exercise their rights and freedoms. The president also appoints the ministers who serve in the cabinet.

The cabinet, also known as the Council of Ministers, oversees and manages government policies. There are currently sixteen ministries in the Colombian cabinet. They include the Ministry of Justice and Law, National Defense, National Education, Mines and Energy, and Foreign Affairs.

President Juan Manuel Santos delivers a speech to the Colombian Congress in 2012.

The Legislature

The Senate and the House of Representatives make up the legislative branch, or Congress, of the Colombian government. Members of Congress are elected to four-year terms. There is no limit on the number of terms a congressperson may serve. There are 102 members of the Senate and 166 members of the House of Representatives.

The two houses are responsible for proposing and approving new laws, amending the constitution, approving treaties, and approving the nation's economic development plans.

Members of the Senate must be more than thirty years old, citizens of the nation, and Colombian by birth. In addition to its joint duties with the House of Representatives, the Senate authorizes the government to declare war, tries government officials accused of wrongdoing, and approves the promotion of military officials.

National Government of Colombia

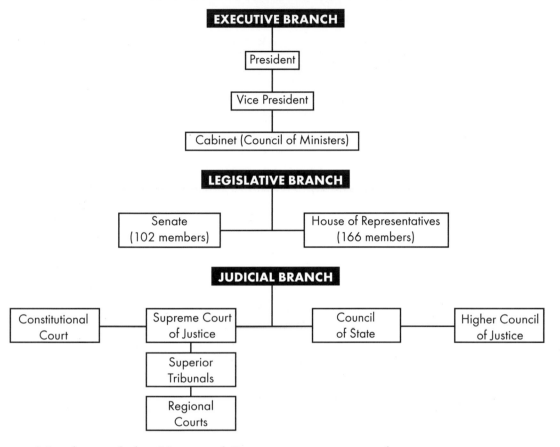

EXECUTIVE BRANCH

President

Vice President

Cabinet (Council of Ministers)

LEGISLATIVE BRANCH

Senate
(102 members)

House of Representatives
(166 members)

JUDICIAL BRANCH

Constitutional
Court

Supreme Court
of Justice

Council
of State

Higher Council
of Justice

Superior
Tribunals

Regional
Courts

Members of the House of Representatives must be more than twenty-five years old and Colombian citizens. The House of Representatives has the extra duties of electing special judges and electing a national spokesperson for human rights.

The Judicial Branch

Most trials in Colombia are held in municipal (city) or regional courts. The country is divided into thirty-three judicial districts. Each has a three-member Superior Tribunal, which reviews decisions made in lower courts.

The Supreme Court of Justice is Colombia's highest judicial body. The court has twenty-three members who are appointed by Congress to eight-year terms. The Supreme Court of Justice is divided into three chambers. One chamber deals with criminal law, one with civil law, and one with labor law. The Supreme Court is the final court of appeal. It also handles cases in which the president or other government or military officials are accused of wrongdoing.

Colombia also has several other specialized courts. The twenty-seven-person Council of State is the highest court on administrative matters. The Constitutional Court consists of

Supreme Court of Justice judges listen to testimony.

The National Anthem

"Himno Nacional de la República de Colombia" ("National Anthem of the Republic of Colombia") is the official name of Colombia's national anthem. Oreste Síndici, an Italian-born Colombian, wrote the music for it in 1887. The lyrics are taken from a poem composed by President Rafael Núñez (below) called "¡Oh gloria inmarcesible!" ("Oh Unfading Glory!"). The anthem was adopted in 1920.

Spanish lyrics

¡Oh gloria inmarcesible!
¡Oh júbilo inmortal!
En surcos de dolores,
el bien germina ya.

¡Cesó la horrible noche!
La libertad sublime
derrama las auroras
de su invencible luz.
La humanidad entera,
que entre cadenas gime,
comprende las palabras
del que murió en la cruz.

English translation

Oh unfading glory!
Oh immortal joy!
In furrows of sorrow,
Good now grows.

The dreadful night is over!
Sublime freedom
Scatters the auroras
Of its invincible light.
The whole of humanity,
In chains wailing,
Understands the words
Of He who died on the cross.

Voters line up to cast their ballots in Bogotá.

nine members who interpret the constitution. The Higher Council of Justice is composed of thirteen members who manage and regulate the country's judicial system.

Regional and Local Government

Colombia is divided into thirty-two departments and the Capitol District of Bogotá. The main function of each department is to oversee economic and social development. The citizens of each department elect a governor and a legislature for that department. Each department has a capital city. The departments are further divided into 1,119 municipalities. A mayor who is elected by the people leads each municipality.

A Visit to Bogotá

Colombia's capital city, Bogotá, was founded in 1538 by Spaniard Gonzalo Jiménez de Quesada. He named the settlement Santa Fé de Bogotá for his hometown of Santa Fe, Spain, and for the site of the settlement, Bacatá, the Muisca capital. In the early eighteenth century, Santa Fé de Bogotá became the capital of the Viceroyalty of New Granada. When Colombia became independent, Bogotá remained the capital.

Bogotá is located on a high plateau in the Cordillera Oriental, at 8,612 feet (2,625 m) above sea level. Because of its high altitude, temperatures remain cool and the city has a pleasant climate throughout the year.

The average daily high temperature in January is 68°F (20°C), and in July it is 66°F (19°C). Average daily low temperatures are similarly consistent, with the temperature typically falling to about 46°F (8°C) in January and 49°F (9°C) in July. The rainiest months are April, May, October, and November.

With a population of 7,102,602, Bogotá is Colombia's largest city. It is also the nation's commercial, cultural, financial, political, and educational center. Bogotá bustles with towering skyscrapers and traffic-jammed streets and highways.

Bogotá is the site of dozens of world-class museums, art galleries, and theaters. The Gold Museum (below), which holds the world's largest collection of pre-Hispanic gold objects, is a top tourist site. The National Museum of Colombia, which focuses on the nation's history and culture, is also popular.

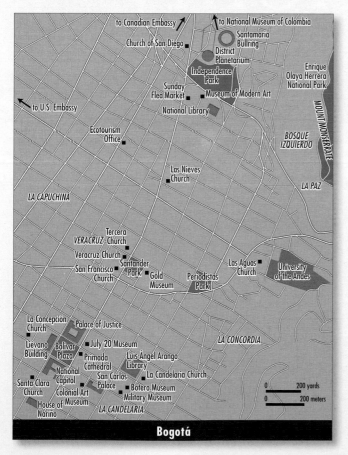

to Canadian Embassy
to National Museum of Colombia
Church of San Diego
Santamaria Bullring
District Planetarium
Independence Park
Enrique Olaya Herrera National Park
Sunday Flea Market
Museum of Modern Art
National Library
to U.S. Embassy
MOUNT MONSERRATE
Ecotourism Office
BOSQUE IZQUIERDO
Las Nieves Church
LA PAZ
LA CAPUCHINA
Tercera Church
VERACRUZ
Veracruz Church
Santander Park
Las Aguas Church
University of the Andes
San Francisco Church
Gold Museum
Periodistas Park
La Concepción Church
Palace of Justice
LA CONCORDIA
Lievano Building
Bolívar Plaza
July 20 Museum
Primada Cathedral
Luis Ángel Arango Library
National Capitol
San Carlos Palace
La Candelaria Church
Santa Clara Church
Colonial Art Museum
Botero Museum
Military Museum
House of Nariño
LA CANDELARIA
0   200 yards
0   200 meters
Bogotá

CHAPTER 6

A Diverse Economy

Today, Colombia has a strong, diverse economy, but this was not always the case. Until the mid-nineteenth century, the country had no major exports to trade for foreign goods. By the 1860s, however, coffee had become the dominant export crop. It remained the foundation of the country's economy until about 1930. During the twentieth century, the country shifted toward industrialization. Coffee revenues were used to buy raw materials and equipment for factories. Today, Colombia is a major exporter of oil, emeralds, textiles, and other products.

Since the early 2000s, the country's economy has generally been improving. In 2012, the nation's gross domestic product (GDP), the total value of all goods and services produced in the country, was growing at an annual rate of 4 percent. More people have been able to find jobs in recent years. Today about 34 percent of the population in Colombia lives below the poverty line. Although this is high, it is down significantly from nearly 50 percent in 2007.

Opposite: **A farmer pours freshly picked coffee beans into a bag. Most Colombian coffee is grown in a small area high in the mountains in the central part of the country.**

Agriculture

About 38 percent of the land in Colombia is used for agriculture. Crops are grown on about 1.4 percent of the land. The rest of the agricultural land is devoted to raising livestock. Colombia produces a wide range of agricultural products. The country's varied climate is able to support crops that thrive in warmer places, such as bananas, and crops that thrive in cooler places, such as potatoes. Agriculture employs 18 percent of Colombia's workforce and accounts for 6.8 percent of the country's GDP.

A worker separates rotten potatoes from good ones. Colombians grow nearly 2 million metric tons of potatoes every year.

In 2011, Colombia produced more than 1.5 billion pounds of coffee. It is the world's third-largest producer of coffee, after Brazil and Vietnam. Most of the coffee Colombia produces is exported to the United States, Germany, France, Japan, and Italy. It is grown mainly on small farms in the northern Andes at altitudes of 4,300 to 6,600 feet (1,300 to 2,000 m).

Colombia's coffee industry has suffered in recent years as world prices have dropped and the climate has changed. In the past thirty years, the temperature in Colombia's coffee-growing regions has risen about 1°F (0.6°C). This increase makes the coffee bean ripen too quickly for the best quality. The higher temperature also provides a breeding ground for coffee rust, a devastating coffee bush disease. As many as half of the country's coffee plantations have been affected.

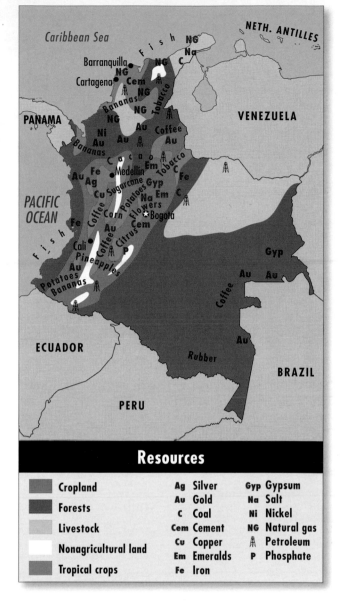

Fresh-cut flowers are Colombia's second-largest agricultural export. The industry is concentrated on the savanna, or treeless plain, near Bogotá. Carnations, orchids, roses, and chrysanthemums are grown and shipped around the world every day. The flower industry employs about one hundred thousand people. An estimated one million people depend

A rancher drives cattle through a field in central Colombia. In 2010, there were 27.8 million cattle in the country.

on the income generated by the flower industry. Colombia is now the second-leading exporter of fresh-cut flowers, after the Netherlands.

Sugarcane is grown in warmer regions, especially in river valleys and on the central Pacific coast. The constant heat and humidity in these areas allow farmers to harvest sugarcane year-round. Major importers of Colombian sugar include Chile, Peru, the United States, and Russia. Other crops grown in Colombia include cotton, tobacco, cacao, corn, rice, wheat, and beans.

Livestock is raised on ranches and farms scattered throughout the country. The river valleys, Caribbean coast, and the Llanos are the major ranching areas. Cattle provide beef and leather. The leather is made into luggage, shoes, and handbags. The items are imported mainly to the United States and Europe. Colombia also has a major dairy industry, producing 7,500,000 metric tons of milk every year.

One of the major problems faced by Colombian cattle ranchers is rustling, or having cattle stolen, by rebel groups. It is estimated that FARC is the country's largest cattle owner. The group steals the cattle and sells it at a low price. This drives the price of livestock down, and decreases the amount of money legal cattle ranchers can earn.

Forestry and Fishing

Forests cover about 55 percent of Colombia. Until the second half of the twentieth century, few roads led into these forests. As roads have been built, however, huge tracts of woodlands have been cut. In recent years, the government and private

Colombian Currency

Colombia's unit of currency is the Colombian peso. Coins come in values of 20, 50, 100, 200, and 500 pesos. Paper money, or banknotes, is issued in denominations of 1,000, 2,000, 5,000, 10,000, 20,000, and 50,000 pesos. In 2013, 1,902 pesos equaled 1 U.S. dollar.

The front of each banknote features an illustration of an important person who contributed to Colombia's history. The reverse side usually depicts a place or an important literary work. The 2,000-pesos banknote features Francisco de Paula Santander, the Colombian military and political leader during the war for independence. The reverse side is an illustration of a doorway of the Casa de Moneda, a museum in Bogotá that was once the mint where coins were made. The 50,000-pesos banknote features Jorge Isaacs, a nineteenth-century Colombian writer, politician, and soldier. The reverse side is a paragraph from María, Isaacs's most important novel. Many people consider María to be the greatest Spanish-language romantic novel ever written.

A fisher casts his net into the Magdalena River. Fish caught in the river include capaz and bocachico.

industry have increased their efforts to replant forest regions where cutting has been heavy.

Colombia has a small fishing industry. Fishers catch mainly tuna, shrimp, and freshwater fish. Most of the country's fishing is done along the coasts and in the Magdalena River. The largest fishing ports are Tumaco and Buenaventura.

Industry

Industry employs about 13 percent of the workforce and accounts for 38 percent of the nation's GDP. The major industrial centers are Bogotá, Medellín, Cali, and Barranquilla. Colombian factories produce chemical products, beverages, cement, automobiles, tires, paper products, and furniture. The Colombian textile industry is based mainly in Medellín. The United States is the largest importer of Colombian apparel and textiles.

What Colombia Grows, Makes, and Mines

AGRICULTURE (2010)

Sugarcane	20,272,600 metric tons
Milk	7,500,000 metric tons
Cattle	27,754,000 animals

MANUFACTURING (VALUE ADDED)

Food products	US$3,471,000,000
Petroleum products	US$2,873,000,000
Beverages	US$1,813,000,000

MINING (2010)

Coal	90,300,000 metric tons
Nickel	70,200 metric tons
Emeralds	5,230,000 carats

Mining

Colombia's rich mineral deposits include gold, nickel, platinum, silver, copper, iron, and bauxite. Salt, limestone, marble, sulfur, and gypsum are also mined. In colonial times, Colombia was a major supplier of gold to Spain. Today it is still an important producer of the valuable metal.

Colombia accounts for roughly 80 percent of the world's emerald production. Most of the emeralds come from mines in the cities of Chivor and Muzo in the mountains around Bogotá. Colombian emeralds are considered the purest emeralds in the world. In some places, poor families dig for emeralds in small local mines or hunt for them in streams or

An oil worker at a refinery in northeastern Colombia. Colombia is the third-largest oil producer in South America, after Venezuela and Brazil.

rivers. They sell the emeralds they find to people who resell them on the international market.

About 450 Colombian emeralds adorn the magnificent Crown of the Andes, a gold crown made in the sixteenth and seventeenth centuries. The crown was made for a statue of Mary, the mother of Jesus Christ, in the Cathedral of Popayán. The statue is larger than life-size.

Energy

Since the late 1980s, Colombia has been an exporter of oil. Today, oil is the country's largest export, accounting for about one-third of all export earnings. Since 2007, production has almost doubled.

The future of Colombia's oil industry is bright. Experts believe Colombia's oil reserves might be enormous, and enough to make the country important in the world oil market. Recent oil discoveries have been made in the basin of the Catatumbo River in the north and along the Caribbean and Pacific regions. One of the world's biggest oil fields was discovered in the Llanos in the 1990s.

Colombia has the largest coal deposits in Latin America and is the world's fifth-largest exporter of coal. The Guajira Peninsula has the country's richest deposits of coal. The coal is mined easily because it is located near the earth's surface. Coal production is anticipated to increase in the coming years as access to the mines is improved. New railway lines are being built that will connect coal-rich areas such as Lenguazaque and Duitama to a river terminal near the city of Barrancabermeja on the Magdalena River. The railways will replace trucks that now have to cross more than 620 miles (1,000 km) of mountain roads to ports on the Caribbean.

System of Weights and Measures

Colombia's main system of weights and measures is the metric system. In this system, the basic unit of length is the meter: 1 meter is equal to 39.4 inches, or 3.3 feet. The basic unit of weight is the kilogram: 1 kilogram, or kilo, is equal to 2.2 pounds.

Colombians also use traditional Spanish weights and measures. The basic units are the *vara* (about 32 inches, or 81 cm), the *libra* (1 pound, or 0.45 kg), and the *arroba* (about 25 pounds, or 11.3 kg).

The coal mine in Cerrejón on the Guajira Peninsula is one of the largest open-pit coal mines in the world.

Colombia's waterways and abundant rainfall contribute significantly to the nation's energy needs. About 70 percent of Colombia's energy comes from hydroelectric power. This is energy generated when rivers turn giant turbines inside dams. Several hydroelectric power plants are located in the area of Bogotá, Cali, and Medellín.

Scientists believe that Colombia's climate and geography provide ideal conditions for other forms of clean, renewable energy. Offshore areas of the Guajira Peninsula experience powerful winds. The Colombian government is currently considering projects to harness wind power there. Solar power is helping to bring power to rural areas where electric power lines are often difficult and costly to set up. The abundance of volcanoes in Colombia

A worker installs solar panels on a house in Colombia. The use of renewable energy sources such as the sun is growing in Colombia.

Most Colombians work in services, such as education.

makes the country a good candidate for geothermal power in the future. Geothermal power uses Earth's heat to create energy, usually with hot water or steam. Several regions where volcanoes are located are being studied for their potential.

Services

Service industries make up the largest part of Colombia's economy. These are industries that provide a service for others, rather than growing or making a product. Service industries include banking, education, health care, sales, and much, much more. Tourism is a growing part of Colombia's economy. In 2003, about half a million foreign tourists visited Colombia. By 2011, three million foreign visitors were arriving every year. This influx of visitors led to new jobs for Colombians, because it created the need for tour guides, taxi drivers, and salespeople, as well as restaurant and hotel workers.

A road winds through the mountains of central Colombia. Because Colombia is so mountainous, travel by road can be difficult.

Today, about 68 percent of Colombians work in service industries. Together, service industries account for 56 percent of the nation's GDP.

Transportation

Colombia's rugged mountains and abundant rivers dominate the terrain of the country. Heavy rainfall in the mountains often causes landslides. Roads and railways are difficult to build and maintain. According to the Colombian government, the nation has about 101,000 miles (163,000 km) of roads, of which 68 percent are paved. Three road systems run north to south between the cordilleras. The Simón Bolívar Highway runs northeast from Guayaquil in Ecuador, through Colombia, to Caracas in Venezuela. Colombia also has about 1,600 miles (2,600 km) of rail lines.

Colombians depend heavily upon waterways for travel. The Magdalena River is the country's major route. At one time, 95 percent of commercial water travel in Colombia occurred on the Magdalena. Today, inland waterway transportation moves 4.2 million tons (3.8 million metric tons) of goods and more than 5.5 million passengers each year.

Colombia's main airline, Avianca, was established in 1919. Its main hub is the El Dorado International Airport in Bogotá, which accounts for almost half of all air traffic in the country. Colombia's most important ports are Barranquilla, Cartagena, and Santa Marta on the Caribbean coast, and Buenaventura and Tumaco on the Pacific coast.

Containers filled with cargo are loaded onto a huge ship in Buenaventura, on the Pacific coast.

CHAPTER 7

The Faces of Colombia

COLOMBIA IS ONE OF THE MOST ETHNICALLY diverse nations in the Western Hemisphere. Roughly 85 different ethnic groups live there. More than half of Colombians are mestizos, people with mixed white European and indigenous ancestry. Afro-Colombians make up about 21 percent of the population. About 20 percent of Colombians are white, the descendants of Spaniards or other European settlers. Indigenous peoples account for 1 percent of the population.

Opposite: **Colombia is a young country. About 26 percent of the people are under age fifteen.**

Mestizos and Whites

Colombia's large mestizo population lives all across the country. It includes many people who live in rural areas of the Andean highlands. Large numbers of mestizos also live in urban areas and form most of the middle and working classes.

In colonial times, Spain discouraged non-Spaniards from immigrating to its colonies, so most early immigrants to Colombia were from Spain. However, in the eighteenth and nineteenth centuries, German, French, and Polish people immigrated to Colombia. Lebanese and Syrian immigrants

People of European descent dominate banking in Colombia. Banker Luis Carlos Sarmiento is the richest man in Colombia, with a net worth of about US$12 billion.

also arrived, with many settling on the Caribbean coast. Traditionally, white Colombians have held the highest positions in government and urban businesses.

Afro-Colombians

People descended from enslaved Africans are called Afro-Colombians. Most Afro-Colombians settled along the Caribbean and Pacific coasts and the Cauca and Magdalena river valleys. They traditionally worked on plantations, on ranches, and in gold mines. Today, the highest concentration of Afro-Colombians is in the Chocó Department on the Pacific coast.

Afro-Colombians face serious economic and social challenges. Many of them work as servants or in the construction industry. Black Colombians are at the forefront of a strong political movement in Colombia to end racism and improve the lives of Afro-Colombians.

Indigenous Colombians

When Spaniards first arrived in Colombia in the early sixteenth century, roughly two million indigenous people inhabited the region. They belonged to more than two hundred different groups and spoke dozens of different languages.

Who Lives in Colombia?	
Mestizo	58%
Afro-Colombian	21%
White	20%
Indigenous	1%

An Afro-Colombian woman dances at a celebration in Cartagena, on the Caribbean coast.

A Guambiano woman carries her child on her back. An estimated twenty-three thousand Guambianos live in Colombia.

Today, most indigenous people live in scattered groups in remote areas of the country. About eighty different groups remain, many speaking their own language. Spanish, however, is the main language spoken by most indigenous people.

The Páez and the Guambianos live in the southern Andean highlands. Population figures are often difficult to confirm, but an estimated 140,000 Páez and Guambianos live in Colombia today. They grow crops such as corn, beans, and yucca using simple wooden tools. They also raise sheep and turkeys. The women weave wool and cotton to make garments for their families and to sell locally. Their homes are made with bamboo wood and thatched roofs. Both men and women wear traditional clothes consisting of a handmade long black skirt, black or gray derby hats, and leather boots. The skirt often has pink trimmings. Women also wear deep blue shawls with a purplish-red fringe and many strings of white beads.

The Wayuu people live on the Guajira Peninsula. They number roughly 122,000. Many Wayuu live as their ancestors did hundreds of years ago. They follow the life of herding and farming. Their traditional homes are built of a mixture of mud, hay, and dried twigs for the walls and cactus for the roofs. Today, cement and other modern building materials are commonly used. Homes are often divided into two rooms in which the residents hang hammocks to sleep. Wayuu settlements typically include five or six houses, which together make up a *ranchería*. The rancherías are usually located far from each other. This helps to prevent herds of livestock from wandering away and mixing with another family's herd.

Wayuu herders travel the hot, dry region with their cattle, goats, and sheep, looking for water and grazing land. Many Wayuu also work as truck drivers, in coal mines, and in the oil fields of Maracaibo, Venezuela.

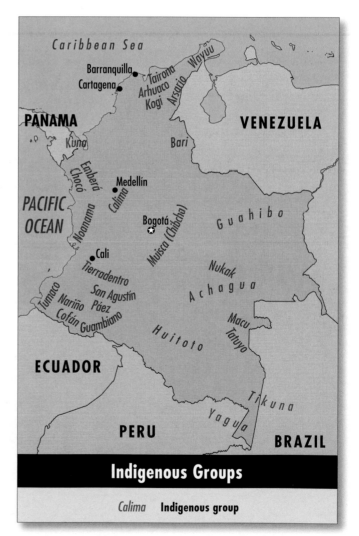

Indigenous Groups

Calima **Indigenous group**

About 10,000 Kogis live in the higher regions of the Santa Marta Mountains. The Kogis are descendants of the Tairona people. The Taironas moved from the Caribbean coast into the mountains when the Spaniards and other indigenous groups invaded their lands.

In present times, some young Kogi people have been making films to document their culture and their political struggles. These documentaries have been shown on Colombian television and at film festivals around the world.

The Kogi people grow potatoes, beans, corn, sugarcane, and fruit. Families keep most of their harvest for themselves.

A group of Kogi priests. Kogi priests are selected at birth and trained from infancy.

Kogi communities trade with others for items such as knives or metal cooking utensils. The Kogis also raise cattle, pigs, sheep, and chickens. Using the tough, durable fiber of the agave plant, they make hammocks and rope. Kogi women also spin wool and cotton into yarn, which the men then weave into fabric. The women make clothing and bags from the fabric. Men wear a tunic and plain, loose-fitting pants tied with a string at the waist. Women wrap a single piece of cloth around their bodies as a dress. The Kogis wear only white clothing, which represents their belief in the purity of nature.

A typical Kogi village contains circular huts made of mud and palm leaves, or stone. Men live apart from the women and children in a hut in the center of the village. Each village has a temple called a *nuhue* where only men are allowed. The leaders are male priests called *mamas*. They make all impor-

Although Kogis usually live in remote villages in the Santa Marta Mountains, they are not completely isolated. Many Kogis go into nearby towns to trade and do other business.

An Endangered People

The Nukak people of Colombia live deep in the tropical rain forest of the Amazon basin. They are expert hunters. They sometimes use blowguns with darts coated in poison to kill monkeys, birds, caimans, and peccaries, members of the pig family. They hunt fish such as catfish, rays, and piranhas, and collect a wide variety of fruit and the honey of twenty species of bees.

Until they were "contacted" by outsiders about twenty-five years ago, the Nukaks lived apart from the larger world. Since then, malaria, measles, and blood diseases brought by a white missionary group and other outsiders have devastated their population. Their numbers have dropped from roughly two thousand in 1988 to about five hundred today.

Recently, the fate of the Nukaks has grown even dimmer. Drug dealers, FARC rebels, and the Colombian army have occupied the Nukaks' tribal lands. Most Nukaks have been forced to live on a plot of land half the size of a football field. Their new home is unsuitable for hunting and fishing. Local farmers will not allow them to hunt in the forests.

The Colombian government has tried to ease the suffering of the Nukaks. It delivers food to them, but it is often not enough. Since leaving the forests, the Nukaks have lost many of their traditional ways. At one time, the Nukaks had no sense of money, but now they are forced to beg for money and other necessities in a nearby town simply to survive.

The Colombian government has promised to enforce the protection of indigenous communities. The Nukaks, however, have little faith in the government. "It is very sad to see our people change their ways so much," says a Nukak man. "Now I'm not sure we could even survive in the jungle, it feels like we are doomed to the modern world."

tant family and community decisions and bring together the villagers to solve larger problems.

Colombia's rain forests are home to many different indigenous groups. The main groups of the Chocó are the Kuna, the Noanama, and the Emberá peoples. Amazon groups include the Yaguas, the Tikunas, and the Cofáns. These peoples have held on to their ancient ways. Indigenous people in the Chocó and the Amazon rely on the resources of the rain forests for survival. They grow corn, peanuts, plantains, and a root plant called manioc. They also hunt monkeys, tapirs, and birds. The people travel the rivers and streams in canoes they make from hollowed-out tree trunks. They catch fish with nets, baskets, and spears they make by hand.

Growing Population

At the beginning of the twentieth century, Colombia's population was only about four million. By the 1960s, the population was booming, with one of the world's highest growth rates: 3.4 percent. Since then, there has been a sharp decline because of family planning. In 2013, the growth rate was 1.1 percent.

Persons per square mile		Persons per square kilometer	
more than 260		more than 100	
131–260		51–100	
66–130		26–50	
25–65		10–25	
3–24		1–9	
fewer than 3		fewer than 1	

Colombians crowd a beach near Cartagena.

Today, more than 45.7 million people live in Colombia. That makes Colombia the third most populous country in Latin America, after Brazil and Mexico. About three-quarters of Colombians live in urban areas. The most populated region is the highlands, home to more than 80 percent of all Colombians.

Language

Spanish is the dominant language in Colombia, spoken by more than 99 percent of the people who live there. Colombian Spanish is closer to the language of Spain than the versions of Spanish spoken in most other Latin American countries. Leaders in Colombia have tried to keep the language pure. That said, there are still many slang words unique to Colombia. For instance, in Colombia, the word *chévere* means "cool" or "good." No one is certain about the origin of this word, but it may come from an African language.

Population of Major Cities (2011 est.)	
Bogotá	7,571,345
Medellín	3,729,970
Cali	3,225,580
Barranquilla	2,185,359
Cartagena	1,492,545

Slang Words in Colombian Spanish

Term	Literal Translation	Meaning
abrirse	to open	to leave
caliente	hot	dangerous
chicharrón	pork rind	a problem to deal with
cojo	wobbly	lacking sense or something weak
embarraria	to cover with mud	to make a serious mistake
fresco	fresh	Be cool!
lobo	wolf	a bad taste
pilas	batteries	wake up, watch out
rata	rat	robber
plata	silver	money
sardino, sardina	sardine	a young person

In addition to Spanish, more than a hundred indigenous languages are also spoken in Colombia. English is common on some Colombian islands in the Caribbean Sea.

This highway worker holds a sign with the word *pare*, which tells drivers to stop.

CHAPTER 8

Freedom to Worship

UNTIL 1991, ROMAN CATHOLICISM WAS COLOMBIA'S official religion. The 1991 constitution, however, changed this and ensured all Colombians the right to worship as they chose. The constitution states, "Freedom of religion is guaranteed. Every individual has the right to freely profess his/her religion and to disseminate it individually or collectively. All religious faiths and churches are equally free before the law."

Today, the vast majority of Colombians consider themselves Roman Catholics. Protestants account for 13.5 percent of the population, with other religions making up 3.6 percent of all Colombians.

Opposite: **Colombians attend an outdoor mass.**

The Roman Catholic Church

The Roman Catholic Church once played a very powerful role in Colombian life. From colonial times to the mid-twentieth century, the church was actively engaged in the nation's political, economic, and social affairs. In politics, the church usually sided with conservatives and wealthy landowners. It opposed the spread of other religions, which were viewed as a threat to its power and influence. By the 1950s, however,

Religious Holidays

Epiphany	January 6
St. Joseph's Day	March 25
Holy Thursday	March or April
Good Friday	March or April
Easter	March or April
Ascension Day	May 9
Corpus Christi	May or June
Feast of Saints Peter and Paul	July 1
Assumption Day	August 15
All Saints' Day	November 1
Immaculate Conception Day	December 8
Christmas	December 25

many Colombian Catholics argued that their faith led them to seek a society that was more equal and helped the poor.

In 1973, the Colombian government and the Vatican, the center of Roman Catholic leadership, agreed to changes that affected the influence of the church. The church agreed

Cathedral of Salt

The Salt Cathedral is a church carved in an old salt mine 600 feet (180 m) beneath the ground. It is located in Zipaquirá, about 30 miles (48 km) north of Bogotá. The original structure was built around 1932 by salt miners who wanted to have a place to pray before starting their day's work. The new cathedral, which opened in 1995, can hold as many as fifteen thousand people. The 75-foot-high (23 m) ceiling towers over a 20-ton (18-metric-ton) block of salt that serves as an altar. An estimated fifty thousand people visit the Salt Cathedral each month.

A priest places ashes on the forehead of a child at a service on Ash Wednesday. This day marks the beginning of Lent, a solemn forty-day period leading up to Easter.

to give up control over public schools and public services for indigenous peoples, and it was banned from censoring public school textbooks.

Although the Catholic Church is not as dominant as it once was, it still influences Colombian life. The church maintains more than seventy-five dioceses, or districts, spread throughout the county. The clergy in Colombia includes about eight thousand priests, more than seventeen thousand nuns, and one thousand brothers (men who devote themselves to the church but are not priests). In many towns and villages, the church, standing in the central plaza, is the most imposing building, overshadowing all others.

The church performs many functions that help the poor and needy. It manages a large network of private schools and universities, social welfare programs, and charitable organizations. The church has also negotiated with rebel groups to help bring peace to the nation's internal conflicts.

Las Lajas Cathedral

The Sanctuary of Our Lady of Las Lajas is a massive Roman Catholic church. It is built on a bridge that spans the canyon of the Guáitara River near Colombia's border with Ecuador. According to local legend, in 1754, a young girl saw an image of Mary, the mother of Jesus, appear on the towering rocks above the bridge. A shrine was built in 1802 to commemorate the event. The shrine was replaced by the current church, which was built between 1916 and 1949. The cliff where the image is said to have appeared forms part of the altar inside the church. The church rises 328 feet (100 m) from the bottom of the canyon.

Protestantism

The first Protestant missionaries arrived in Colombia in the mid-1800s. In the 1950s, Protestants accounted for less than 1 percent of the entire population. Since then, Protestantism has grown considerably in Colombia. Evangelical and Pentecostal Protestant groups have been particularly successful with the working class and the lower middle class.

Colombia's Religions

Roman Catholicism	81%
Protestantism	13.5%
No religious belief	1.9%
Other faiths (Judaism, Bahaism, Seventh-Day Adventist, Mormonism, Jehovah's Witness)	3.6%

Other Religions

Other religious groups represented in Colombia include Mormons, Seventh-Day Adventists, and Jehovah's Witnesses. The first Mormons in Colombia were from North America, and they met in prayer groups in Cali and Bogotá. In 1966, the first missionaries arrived in the country. Today, there are an estimated 180,500 Mormons in Colombia. Seventh-Day Adventists number roughly 130,000, while Jehovah's Witnesses account for 126,500 people.

There are about 7,000 Jews in Colombia. The first Jews settled in the area during the sixteenth century, when many came to Latin America to escape religious persecution in Spain. More Jews arrived in Colombia in the 1880s from the Middle East and in the 1930s and 1940s from Europe. The largest population of Jews lives in Bogotá. There are also communities in Cali, Barranquilla, and Medellín.

Colombia also has small numbers of Buddhists, Hindus, Baha'is, Taoists, and Muslims. The city of Maicao in the Guajira Peninsula is home to Latin America's second-largest mosque, or Muslim house of worship, the Mosque of Omar Ibn Al-Khattab.

Several indigenous groups, including the Kuna, Macu, Kogi, and Tatuyo peoples, continue to practice their ancestral faiths. Some descendants of enslaved people who lived along the Caribbean and Pacific coasts practice African forms of worship.

Protestant Colombians gather for a prayer service.

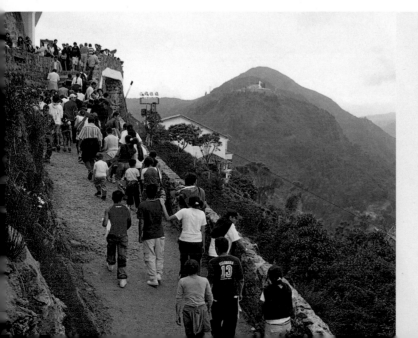

Mount Monserrate

A popular religious site in Bogotá is Mount Monserrate, a sanctuary located 10,341 feet (3,152 m) above sea level. The sanctuary was built between 1650 and 1657. Visitors climb a long, winding mountain path to visit a statue of Jesus Christ called El Señor Caído (The Fallen Lord). Highly religious people often make the pilgrimage on their knees. Less active visitors can take an aerial tramway to the top of the hill and enjoy the beautiful views of the city below when they arrive.

CHAPTER 9

The Soul
of a People

COLOMBIA'S RICH ARTISTIC HERITAGE IS A BLEND of its diverse regional and ethnic identities. For many years, Colombian culture was closely related to Spanish culture. Spanish art and design influenced Colombia's architecture. Spanish literature shaped the styles and themes of Colombian writers. In the twentieth century, Colombia showed the world its own unique artistic traditions. Colombians made important contributions in literature, art and architecture, world music, theater, and sports.

Opposite: **A drummer performs at a Colombia Independence Day event.**

Art and Sculpture

Colombia had an artistic heritage all its own before it was exposed to outside influences. Hundreds of years before the Spaniards arrived, indigenous peoples were crafting detailed works of gold, silver, and gemstones. During the colonial period, colonists brought a European influence to their new country. In the late eighteenth century, Spanish physician José Celestino Mutis created more than 5,300 drawings depicting Colombia's natural beauty. His collection of drawings, which included animals, plants, and landscapes, provided a firsthand guide to the wonders of New Granada.

Nineteenth-century Colombian artists often painted scenes telling the story of the country's independence. Pedro José Figueroa and José María Espinosa produced many works of Simón Bolívar, considered the father of Colombia. Policarpa Salavarrieta, the spy who worked for the independence movement, was also a popular subject.

Pedro Nel Gómez and Débora Arango, painters from Medellín, made important contributions to Colombian art in the twentieth century. Gómez painted huge murals that showed daily life in Medellín. He depicted scenes of workers, gold production, family, and violence. His works decorate several government buildings in his hometown. Arango created highly political art, often criticizing the government or the Roman Catholic Church.

National Museum of Colombia

The National Museum of Colombia, located in downtown Bogotá, is the country's largest and oldest museum. Built in 1823, the massive, stone wall building served as a prison until 1946. The museum features more than twenty thousand objects and pieces of art highlighting different periods of the country's history, from 10,000 BCE to the present. Artifacts from early times include gold and silver ornaments, ancient pottery and figurines, and tools. Paintings by Colombian masters such as Fernando Botero, Débora Arango, and Santiago Martínez Delgado are also on display.

Colombia's most famous artist today is Fernando Botero, who was born in 1932 in Medellín. He studied in New York and Europe. His paintings and sculptures often feature chubby figures with simple expressions. His work frequently pokes fun at the government and the military.

Edgar Negret, born in 1920 in Popayán, is one of Colombia's best-known sculptors. One of his most important works is *Dinamismo*, a long, red steel sculpture that appears outside the entrance to a bank in Bogotá. Another notable Colombian sculptor is Eduardo Ramírez Villamizar, who was born in 1922 in Pamplona, Colombia. Ramírez Villamizar created a sculpture in honor of U.S. president John F. Kennedy that is on display in Washington, D.C. One of Colombia's most

The sculptures of Fernando Botero can be found all over the world. *The Cat* is in Barcelona, Spain.

important modern sculptors is Doris Salcedo. She transforms everyday objects into powerful pieces that represent the experiences of immigrants, victims of war, and others who are often ignored.

The works of Gabriel García Márquez helped spark the boom of South American literature.

Literature

One of the most important authors in all of Latin America is the Colombian Gabriel García Márquez. He was born in Aracataca, close to the Santa Marta Mountains, in 1928. In 1982 he was awarded the Nobel Prize in Literature, the world's highest literary award, for *One Hundred Years of Solitude*. García Márquez is the only Colombian ever to win this literary honor. In this major work, he writes about several generations of the same family in a town called Macondo. Through this one family and town, García Márquez is able to explore Colombian history and life. Much of his work is in a style called magical realism, in which magical elements occasionally appear in what are otherwise completely realistic worlds. García

Márquez's other well-known novels include *Love in the Time of Cholera*, based on a family romance, and *The Autumn of the Patriarch*, about a South American dictator.

Other major Colombian writers include Laura Restrepo and Fernando Vallejo. Restrepo, a former journalist, tells dramatic stories of people in difficult situations combined with carefully researched details. Vallejo is one of the most controversial authors in Colombia. His novel *Our Lady of the Assassins* is a tale of teenagers hired by Medellín drug dealers to be assassins. Vallejo's strong political views led him to give up his Colombian

Fernando Vallejo is both a novelist and a filmmaker.

A Great Modern Novelist

Laura Restrepo is one of the great figures of modern Colombian literature. She was born in Bogotá in 1950. Restrepo became politically active in Spain and in Argentina, where she was part of a rebel movement that opposed Argentina's military dictatorship. When she returned to Colombia, she became a journalist.

In 1982, Restrepo was named to a committee engaged in peace talks with the M-19, a rebel group that made peace with the government in 1990. As a result, she received death threats from the rebels and fled to Mexico for six years. Her book *Story of a Fascination* provides a firsthand account of her experiences during the peace negotiations.

Restrepo frequently sets her novels in Colombia during times of chaos and political turmoil. She focuses on her characters' struggles to survive in a country torn apart by violence. *Leopard in the Sun* tells the story of a war between two families involved in the Colombian drug trade.

Restrepo has won many international awards for her writing. She continues to be outspoken on issues that affect Colombian society today.

citizenship after the reelection of President Álvaro Uribe Vélez in 2006, because he disagreed with Uribe's policies.

José Asunción Silva, one of Colombia's greatest poets, was born into a wealthy family in Bogotá in 1865. As an adult, he traveled through Europe, where he met many writers. He wrote romantic, sentimental poetry, often about his sister whose death sent him into a great depression. Jorge Artel, another great Colombian poet, gave voice to the experience of Afro-Colombians in the twentieth century.

Theater

Until the mid-twentieth century, Colombian theater was mainly for the rich. Plays usually focused on themes of religion and supported the Roman Catholic Church. In the mid-1950s, however, a new journal called *Mito* began publishing Europe's leading thinkers in the fields of culture, literature, and theater. The popularity of the magazine led to the birth of modern Colombian theater.

Inspired by the trends he read about in *Mito*, Enrique Buenaventura founded an influential theater group in Cali. He also became one of the most important Colombian playwrights and theater directors in Latin America. His production of *Documents from Hell* was a series of one-act plays that explored human rights conditions in Colombia. Buenaventura helped bring theater to a wider audience in Colombia and encouraged other playwrights to write about important social issues.

Music

The most popular style of Colombian music is called *cumbia*. The rhythms and dance of cumbia originally came from West Africa. In Colombia, cumbia developed with the Afro-Colombians living along the Atlantic and Pacific coasts. The most common instruments played in cumbia are drums, claves (two short sticks that are struck to produce a clicking sound), maracas, clarinet, accordion, and flute.

Vallenato (born in the valley) originated near the north coast as a type of folk poetry put to music. It became popular among working and lower middle-class people at parties and celebrations. The sad-sounding vallenato music is often set to love stories and dramatic tales. The music is played on a small drum called a *caja vallenata* and a *guacharaca*, a wooden tube that is rubbed with a metal fork. Accordions are often used to accompany vallenato.

Many Colombians also listen to pop and rock music. A homegrown favorite is singer, songwriter, and dancer Shakira, who was born in Barranquilla. Shakira has produced records in

Cumbia arose from a mix of African, indigenous, and Spanish music.

both English and Spanish, and her albums mix pop, rock, and folk music. Her best-selling songs include "Hips Don't Lie" and "Whenever, Wherever."

Sports

Soccer is the most popular sport in Colombia. The Colombian national team's greatest victory was in 1993, when the team defeated Argentina 5–0. The victory came as a complete surprise to soccer fans around the world: Argentina had won thirty-three straight games before the match with Colombia!

Cycling is also a beloved sport in Colombia. Colombian racers often place high in the rankings in major cycling events held around the world. Luis "Lucho" Herrera won the 1987 Tour of Spain, a race through Spain that takes three weeks. That same year he also finished fifth overall at the Tour de France, the world's most prestigious cycling event. Colombia's mountains, valleys, and steep winding roads provide cyclists with ideal training conditions.

By 2013, Shakira had won two Grammy Awards and eight Latin Grammy Awards.

A player prepares for a throw in a tejo practice.

Before the arrival of the Spaniards, indigenous Colombians played a game called *tejo*. Today, a version of the game remains popular in Colombia. To play the game, players throw a metal disc from a distance into a box packed with small gunpowder caps. When the disc hits a cap, a small explosion occurs. The player who hits the most caps wins.

At the Olympics

Colombia first sent athletes to the Summer Olympics in 1932. Since then, Colombian athletes have taken part in every Summer Olympics except the 1952 games. The size of the Olympic team from Colombia has been increasing steadily. In 2012, 104 Colombian athletes competed in the games in London, England. It was Colombia's most successful Olympics ever. Colombians took home eight medals, including Mariana Pajón's gold medal in women's BMX cycling.

Colombia's strongest events have traditionally been cycling and weight lifting, but in 2012 Colombians also won medals in the triple jump (a track-and-field event), judo, tae kwon do, and wrestling. When the medal winners returned home to Colombia, they were welcomed as heroes in Bogotá. Thousands of people gathered in the streets to celebrate their victory and thank them for representing Colombia at the Games.

Mariana Pajón (left) was the second Colombian to win an Olympic gold medal. The first was weight lifter María Isabel Urrutia in the 2000 games.

CHAPTER 10

Daily Life

EACH REGION IN COLOMBIA OFFERS A DIFFERENT way of life for the people who live there. In the cities, middle-class Colombians live like they do in the United States. They work as doctors, lawyers, and businesspeople. Others work in factories and warehouses. Some sell jewelry, books, and leather goods from small street stalls.

In mountain regions, many people work on coffee plantations. Along the coasts, people work in fishing villages and harbors. Those who stay ashore might load and unload cargo at the docks. On the eastern Llanos, cowboys tend to their herds and raise pigs, goats, sheep, and other livestock.

Family Life

The family is the most important social unit in Colombia. Children typically live with their parents until they marry. As in North America, however, young adults who are working

Opposite: **A family rides a motorbike through Leticia, in southern Colombia.**

often get their own apartments before marriage. It is common for newly married couples to live with their families until they can afford a home of their own.

Colombian families tend to be very tight-knit. Parents, children, grandparents, aunts, uncles, and cousins often live together in the same home. Family members support one another. Frequently, when a Colombian moves to another country, he or she will send money to the family to help it out.

Today, the roles of men and women in Colombian society are changing. Traditionally, men were considered the head of the family and worked to earn a living. For centuries, wealthy families have employed servants, and poor women have worked cooking and cleaning in the homes of other people. Women cooked and took care of the home and children. In recent years, more middle-class Colombian women are working outside the home to help support the family. Many upper-class women enter professional fields or run for political office.

A Colombian grandmother and child. Colombians live an average of seventy-five years.

Housing

Housing in Colombia varies greatly, depending upon the location and income of the resident. In cities, middle-class and working-class people live in apartment buildings. The wealthy live in colonial mansions or modern ranch houses. The poor often live in slums on the outskirts of cities. Their houses often lack running water and electricity.

This scientist is studying mosquitoes. More Colombian women than men attend college.

Taking It to the Streets

The capital city of Bogotá has been closing its traffic-congested main streets every Sunday and national holiday since 1974. On these days, Bogotá residents and tourists may do whatever they want on the roads: walk, run, bike, skate, skateboard, skip, or hop. The policy is in effect from 7:00 a.m. to 2:00 p.m. and affects more than 75 miles (120 km) of paved roads.

Poor families in Colombia build their homes from whatever materials they can find.

In remote regions, some people live in simple homes built on stilts that hold the house above the ground. This prevents wildlife from entering the houses.

Education

Colombia has a literacy rate of 90 percent. Free education is available to everyone. Children between the ages of six and sixteen must attend school. Many young people—especially poor

Tingo, Tingo, Tango!

Children in Colombia enjoy playing a game called Tingo, Tingo, Tango. All the players stand in a circle except for the player who is "it." The person who is "it" closes his or her eyes and says, "Tingo, tingo, tingo, tingo." Meanwhile, the other players pass a small object around the circle from one to the next. The player who is "it" then calls out "Tango!" The player who is holding the object at that moment must perform an act that "it" chooses. He or she might be asked to do a silly walk, crow like a rooster, or crawl around the circle. The player who was caught becomes "it" for the next game.

children in cities and those who work on a family farm—do not complete their education, or do not attend school at all.

Students at many schools in Colombia are required to wear uniforms.

The school year runs from February to November in the capital city of Bogotá. In other places, it runs from August to June. Instruction is in Spanish, but some private schools conduct their classes in English, German, or French. Many schools in rural areas suffer from a lack of teachers, books, classrooms, and equipment.

High school students who complete their studies and pass a special examination may attend college. There are more than one hundred public and private universities in Colombia. Major universities include the National University of Colombia, which has branches in several cities, the University of the Andes in Bogotá, the University of Antioquia in Medellín, and the University of Valle in Cali.

National Holidays

New Year's Day	January 1
Labor Day	May 1
Declaration of Independence	July 20
Battle of Boyacá	August 7
Columbus Day	October 12
Independence of Cartagena	November 11

Festivals

Celebrations are an important part of daily life in Colombia. The most famous are the Carnival of Blacks and Whites and the Barranquilla Carnival.

In Popayán, during the first week of January, there is a festival to celebrate the end of the Christmas season. *Día de Negritos* (Day of the Black Ones) is celebrated on January 5. *Fiesta de los Blanquitos* (Festival of the White Ones) is held the next day. On Día de Negritos, boys chase girls and try to smear them with black shoe polish. Street parades are held in the afternoon. Strolling bands of colorfully dressed musicians provide the entertainment. On Fiesta de los Blanquitos, boys run through the streets tossing white flour or talcum powder

A Special Birthday

In Spanish, the word quince means "fifteen." A girl who is turning fifteen years of age is a *quinceañera*. In Colombia, that event is celebrated with a special party. The party is called the Fiesta de Quince, or the quinceañera, and marks the young girl's arrival into womanhood.

Almost every family, rich or poor, tries to make the fiesta a day to remember. Most quinceañeras receive a special dress for the occasion. Each quinceañera is also given a special present that she will keep for her lifetime. Jewelry, such as a ring or necklace, is commonly given. Wealthier families might additionally give computers or vacation trips. A cake, similar to a wedding cake, and heaps of tasty food are served at the fiesta. The first dance of the night, a waltz, is for the quinceañera and her father.

on people. Others join in and pour water on those covered in flour until everyone is covered in a sticky paste. Thousands of people participate in the grand parade, cheering and throwing confetti, while dancing to traditional Colombian music.

The Barranquilla Carnival is a joyous time to have fun before the solemn period of Lent, the forty days before Easter. For several days, the city's inhabitants and tourists from around the world celebrate with music and parades. Colorful floats, dancers, costumed groups, and fire-breathers fill the streets in Colombia's largest celebration.

The Barranquilla Carnival features parades with floats and colorfully dressed dancers.

Food

Meals in Colombia often begin with soup. *Ajiaco*, which originated in Bogotá, is now popular throughout the country. This hearty soup is made with chicken, potatoes, corn, and avocado. *Sancocho*, a traditional soup from Cali, is made with chicken, corn, plantains (starchy bananas), and a variety of seasonings. *Changua* is a favorite Andean soup. It is made from beef broth, milk, and coriander. *Sopa de pan* is a main course soup made with bread, eggs, and cheese.

Tasty breads are served with most Colombian meals. *Almojábanas* are cheesy rolls. *Arepa* is a flatbread made with ground corn and salt, and is rolled out and lightly toasted on a griddle.

Ajiaco is a filling soup sometimes made with three different kinds of potatoes.

Let's Make Arepas

Colombians eat arepas with almost every meal. Arepas are easy to make, but you'll need masarepa cornmeal. Have an adult help you with this recipe.

Ingredients

1 ½ cups masarepa cornmeal

1 teaspoon salt

2 ¾ cups hot water

2 tablespoons butter, melted

Vegetable oil

Directions

Combine the masarepa cornmeal and the salt in a large bowl. Pour the hot water over the cornmeal and mix it in thoroughly. Stir in the butter. Then cover the dough with plastic wrap and let it sit for about 15 minutes.

Divide the dough into about 20 balls. Flatten each one until it is about ¼ inch thick. Pour ½ tablespoon of oil into a frying pan, and then place a few balls of dough in the pan. Cook the arepas over medium heat for about 5 minutes on each side, until they are slightly browned. Add more oil to the pan before cooking the next round of arepas. Serve piping hot. Enjoy!

Colombians drink less than half as much coffee as Americans drink.

Chorizos and *empanadas* are among the most popular Colombian dishes. Chorizos are heavily seasoned sausages. Empanadas are pastries filled with meat, chicken, and vegetables. *Bandeja paisa* is a favorite meal in Antioquia. This dish is made with red beans, *chicharrón* (fried pork skin), beef, rice, plantains, and avocado, and served with pieces of the flatbread arepa.

Known around the world for its fine coffee, Colombia offers many varieties of the beverage. *Tinto*, a small, strong cup heavily sweetened with sugar, is very popular. Other favorite coffee drinks include *café con leche* (half coffee, half milk) and *pintado* (coffee with a bit of milk).

Looking Ahead

Colombia has been forced to face many problems over the years. Violence, poverty, and the illegal drug trade have devastated many regions of the country. Yet Colombia also has many treasures. It has been blessed with incredible natural beauty, from thick, lush rain forests to soaring, snowcapped mountains. The country's rich heritage blends indigenous, African, and European cultures. Colombia's greatest blessing is its warm and hopeful people. Today, they look ahead with confidence and optimism to a promising future.

A woman tosses flowers at the Festival of the Flowers in Medellín.

Timeline

COLOMBIAN HISTORY

The territories of New Granada win their independence; the Republic of Gran Colombia is founded.	**1819**
Venezuela and Ecuador split from Gran Colombia; Colombia and Panama become the Republic of New Granada.	**1830**
The country is renamed the United States of Colombia, or simply, Colombia.	**1863**
The War of a Thousand Days results in almost 100,000 deaths.	**1899–1902**
Panama declares its independence from Colombia.	**1903**
Bloody conflict rages through Colombia; more than 200,000 people die in what is known as *La Violencia*.	**1948–1962**
Conservatives and liberals jointly form the National Front to govern Colombia.	**1958**
Rebel groups begin fighting the government; the illegal drug trade grows large.	**1960s**
The National Front is disbanded.	**1974**
Writer Gabriel García Márquez wins the Nobel Prize in Literature.	**1982**
Mount Ruiz volcano erupts, killing more than 25,000 people.	**1985**
The present constitution is adopted.	**1991**
President Andrés Pastrana Arango introduces Plan Colombia to end the armed conflict with rebels.	**1999**
Efforts to slow the drug trade show signs of success.	**Early 2000s**
Progress is made in negotiations between FARC and the Colombian government.	**2013**

WORLD HISTORY

1865	The American Civil War ends.
1879	The first practical lightbulb is invented.
1914	World War I begins.
1917	The Bolshevik Revolution brings communism to Russia.
1929	A worldwide economic depression begins.
1939	World War II begins.
1945	World War II ends.
1969	Humans land on the Moon.
1975	The Vietnam War ends.
1989	The Berlin Wall is torn down as communism crumbles in Eastern Europe.
1991	The Soviet Union breaks into separate states.
2001	Terrorists attack the World Trade Center in New York City and the Pentagon near Washington, D.C.
2004	A tsunami in the Indian Ocean destroys coastlines in Africa, India, and Southeast Asia.
2008	The United States elects its first African American president

Fast Facts

Official name:	Republic of Colombia
Capital:	Bogotá
Official language:	Spanish

Medellín

Colombian flag

Puracé National Natural Park

Year of founding:	1819
Founder:	Simón Bolívar
National anthem:	"Himno Nacional de la República de Colombia" ("National Anthem of the Republic of Colombia")
Form of government:	Republic
Head of state:	President
Head of government:	President
Area of country:	439,736 square miles (1,138,911 sq km)
Latitude and longitude of geographic center:	3°45' N, 73° W
Bordering countries:	Venezuela to the northeast, Brazil to the east and southeast, Peru to the south, Ecuador to the southwest, and Panama to the northwest
Highest elevation:	Cristóbal Colón, 18,946 feet (5,775 m) above sea level
Lowest elevation:	Sea level, along the coasts
Average high temperature:	In January, 68°F (20°C) in Bogotá, 90°F (32°C) in Cali; in July, 66°F (19°C) in Bogotá, 91°F (33°C) in Cali
Average low temperature:	In January, 46°F (8°C) in Bogotá, 62°F (17°C) in Cali; in July, 49°F (9°C) in Bogotá, 60°F (15°C) in Cali
Average annual rainfall:	118 inches (300 cm) countrywide; 300 inches (760 cm) in the rain forest;10 inches (25 cm) on the Guajira Peninsula

Las Lajas Cathedral

National population (2013 est.):	45,745,783

Population of major cities (2011 est.):

Bogotá	7,571,345
Medellín	3,729,970
Cali	3,225,580
Barranquilla	2,185,359
Cartagena	1,492,545

Landmarks:
- ▶ *Gold Museum*, Bogotá
- ▶ *Las Lajas Cathedral*, Ipiales
- ▶ *San Felipe de Barajas Castle*, Cartagena
- ▶ *San Agustín Archaeological Park*, San Agustín
- ▶ *Puracé National Natural Park*, Popayán

Economy: Colombia is one of the world's largest producers of coffee. It is also a major exporter of fresh-cut flowers and sugarcane. The country has large cattle and dairy industries. Major manufactured products include textiles, wood and metal products, chemicals, cement, foods and beverages, transportation equipment, and machinery. About 90 percent of the world's emeralds come from Colombia. Nickel, gold, and silver are also mined there. Oil and coal are important exports.

Currency: The Colombian peso. In 2013, 1,902 pesos equaled 1 U.S. dollar.

System of weights and measures: Colombians use both the metric system and traditional Spanish weights and measures.

Literacy rate (2012): 90.4%

Currency

Schoolchildren

Shakira

Common Spanish words and phrases:

Hola	Hello
Buenas tardes	Good afternoon
¡Que tenga suerte!	Good luck!
¿Cómo estás?	How are you?
Gracias	Thank you
Por favor	Please
¿Cuánto?	How much?
¿Cuántos?	How many?
¿Hablas Español?	Do you speak Spanish?
Me llamo . . .	My name is . . .
¿De dónde eres?	Where are you from?
Vivo en los Estados Unidos	I live in the United States

Prominent Colombians:

Fernando Botero (1932–)
Artist

Pedro Nel Gómez (1899–1984)
Muralist

Juan Manuel Santos (1951–)
President

Gabriel García Márquez (1928–)
Writer and Nobel Prize winner

Laura Restrepo (1950–)
Writer and journalist

Francisco de Paula Santander (1792–1840)
Military leader and president

Policarpa Salavarrieta (ca. 1795–1817)
Spy for independence movement

Shakira (1977–)
Singer

To Find Out More

Books

▶ Blackford, Cheryl. *Colombia.* Minneapolis: Lerner, 2012.

▶ DuBois, Jill, Leslie Jermyn, and Yong Jui Lin. *Colombia.* Tarrytown, NY: Marshall Cavendish, 2011.

▶ Sheen, Barbara. *Foods of Colombia.* Detroit: KidHaven Press, 2012.

DVDs

▶ *Ancient Voices, Modern World: Colombia & Amazon.* National Geographic, 2010.

▶ *Guerrilla Gold Rush.* National Geographic, 2013.

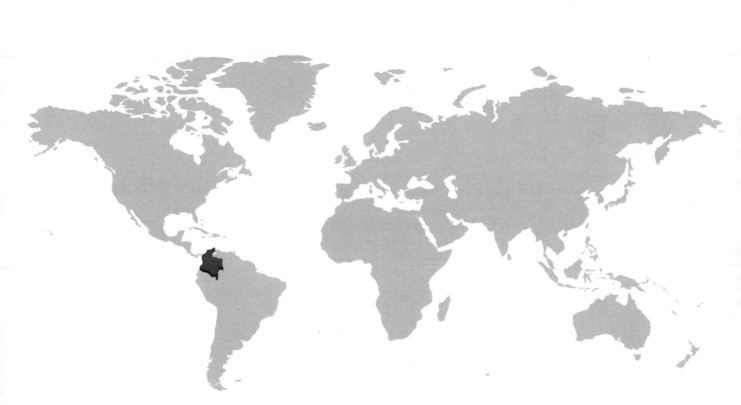

▶ Visit this Scholastic Web site for more information on Colombia:
www.factsfornow.scholastic.com
Enter the keyword **Colombia**

Index

Page numbers in *italics*
indicate illustrations.

hydroelectric power in, 82
independence and, 49
Jewish people in, 103
Laura Restrepo and, 110
libraries in, 9
location of, 24, 71
manufacturing in, 78
Mormon Church in, 102
Mount Monserrate, 103, *103*
National Museum of Colombia,
    71, 106, *106*
Olympic athletes in, 115
population of, 16, 29, *46*, 71, 96
protests in, *59*
roadways, 119, *119*
universities in, 9
Viceroyalty of New Granada and, 47
Bolívar, Simón, 49, 50, 106
borders, 15, 18, 20, 22, 23, 52
Botero, Fernando, 106, 107, *107*, 133
Buenaventura, Enrique, 111
butterflies, 21

C

Cali. *See also* cities.
    climate, 16
    coffee industry in, 29
    elevation of, 19, 29
    Ermita Church, 29, *29*
    founding of, 29, 45
    hydroelectric power in, 82
    Jewish people in, 103
    La Plaza de Toros de Cañaveralejo,
        29
    location of, 24, 29
    manufacturing in, 78
    Mormons in, 102
    population, 29, 96
    Sebastián de Belalcázar and, 29,
        45, *45*
    sugar industry in, 29
    theater in, 111

tourism in, 29
Calima people, 42
Caño Cristales, 24, *24*
capital city. *See* Bogota.
Capitol District of Bogotá, 70
Caribbean Lowlands, 15, 20–21, *20*
Caribbean Sea, *14*, 15, 21, *25*, *52*
Carnival of Blacks and Whites, 122
carnivals, 122–123, *123*
Cartagena
    architecture, 9, 48, *48*
    Bartolomé Calvo Library, 48
    Church of San Pedro Claver, 48, *48*
    founding of, 48
    independent government of, 49
    indigenous people and, 48
    Museum of Modern Art, 29, 48
    Naval Museum, 48
    Naval School, 65
    Old Town, 48
    Palace of the Inquisition in Bolívar
        Plaza, 48
    Plaza de los Coches, 48
    population of, 8, 96
    port of, 85
    San Felipe de Barajas Castle, 48
    Torre del Reloj, 48, *48*
    tourism in, 13, 48
Casa de Moneda, 77
Catatumbo River, 81
Cathedral of Popayán, 80
Cattley, William, 38
Cauca River, 24, 34
children, 47, *60*, 86, *90*, *118*, *121*
Chingaza National Park, 33
Chocó region, 21, *21*, 28, 88, 95
Church of San Pedro Claver, 48, *48*
cities. *See also* Barranquilla; Bogotá;
    Cali; Cartagena; Medellín; towns;
    villages.
    Barrancabermeja, 81
    Buenaventura, 26, 78, *85*

Chivor, 79
Leticia, *116*
Magangué, 24
Maicao, 103
Muzo, 79
Quibdó, 22
Santa Marta, 43, 85
Tumaco, 20, 78
Zipaquirá, 100
civil wars, 50
climate, 16, 22, 27–28, *27*, 29, 31, 71,
    74, 75
clothing, 90–91, 93, *121*
coal mining, 81, *81*, 91
coastline, 13, *14*, 16, 17, 96
cocaine trade, 11–12, *11*, 12–13, 59
Cofán people, 95
coffee industry, 53, 54, *72*, 73, 75,
    117, 126, *126*
Colombian Independence Day, 49
Colombian peso (currency), 51, 77, *77*
Columbus, Christopher, 15
Comunero Revolt, 49
constitution, 52, 63, 68, 70, 99
Constitutional Court, 68, 70
construction industry, 88
coral reefs, 26
Cordillera Central, 18–19, 23, 24, 34,
    35, 41
Cordillera Occidental, 19, 21, 22, 24
Cordillera Oriental, 17, 18, 23, 24, 33,
    41, 71
Cosa, Juan de la, 43
cotton, 21
Council of Ministers, *64*, 65
Council of State, 68
crime rate, 13
Cristóbal Colón, 16, 18
Crown of the Andes, 80
Cundinamarca, 49
currency (Colombian peso), 51, 77, *77*
cycling, 113

D

dairy farming, 79
Day of the Colombian Woman, 51
deserts, 36, *36*
diseases, 94
drug trade, 11–12, *11*, 12–13, 57–59, *57, 58*, 60, 94
Duitama, 81

E

earthquakes, 20
earthworms, 32
economy
  agriculture and, 54, 74–77
  banana industry, 21, 54, 74
  coffee industry, *53*, 54, *72*, 73, 75, 117, 126, *126*
  construction industry, 88
  currency (Colombian peso), 51, 77, *77*
  drug trade, 11–12, 57–58
  employment, *53*, 74, *74*, 75–76, *82*, 83–84, *83*, 91, 117
  exports, 73, 75, 76, 78, 79
  fishing industry, 78, *78*, 117
  flower industry, 75–76
  foreign aid, 59
  forestry, 77–78
  gross domestic product (GDP), 73, 74, 78
  manufacturing, 73, 78, 79
  mining, 24, 47, 79–80, 81, *81*, 91
  National Front, 56
  oil industry, 22, 80–81, *80*, 91
  rebel groups and, 10
  service industries, 83–84, *83*
  sugarcane, 79
  tourism and, 13, 83
  War of a Thousand Days, 53
Ecuador, 15, 18, 19, 20, 45, 47, 50, 60–61, 84, 102

education, 9, 13, 83, *83*, 101, *119*, 120–121, *121*
El Cocuy National Park, 17
El Dorado ceremony, 44
El Dorado International Airport, 85
elections, 54, 61, 63, 65, 66, *70*, 110
elevation, 16, 17, *17*, 18–19, 22, 27
El Señor Caído (The Fallen Lord) statue, 103
Emberá people, 95
emerald mining, 79–80
employment, *53*, 74, *74*, 75–76, *82*, 83–84, *83*, 91, 117
encomienda system, 46–47
energy, 80–83, *82*, 119
English language, 97, 121
Ermita Church, 29, *29*
Espinosa, José María, 106
European exploration, 39, 43, *43*, 45
European immigrants, 87–88, *88*
European settlers, 35, 43, 45–46, *45*, 47, 71, 92, 105
executive branch of government, 12, 63–65, 67, 69, *69*
exports, 73, 75, 76, 78, 79

F

families, *90*, *116*, 117–118, *118*
FARC. *See* Revolutionary Armed Forces of Colombia.
Federmann, Nikolaus, 45
Ferdinand VII, king of Spain, 49
festivals, 122–123, *123*, *127*
Fiesta de Quince, 122
Figueroa, Pedro José, 106
fishing industry, 78, *78*, 117
flower industry, 75–76
foods, 124, *124*, 125, *125*, 126
forestry, 77–78

G

Gaitán, Jorge Eliécer, 54
García Márquez, Gabriel, 108–109, *108*, 133
geothermal power, 82–83
gold, 42, 43, 44, *44*, 47, 79, 80
Gold Museum, 71, *71*
Gómez, Laureano, 55
Gómez, Pedro Nel, 106, 133
Gorgona Island, 26, *26*
government
  civil wars, 50
  conservatives, 50, 52, 54, 55, 56, 57, 65, 99
  constitution, 52, 63, 66, 68, 70, 99
  Constitutional Court, 68, 70
  Council of Ministers, *64*, 65
  Council of State, 68
  dictatorships, 55
  drug trade and, 12–13, 57, 58, 59, 60
  elections, 54, 61, 63, 65, 66, *70*, 110
  executive branch, 12, 63–65, 67, 69, *69*
  Higher Council of Justice, 70
  House of Representatives, 66, 67
  independence, 49–50, 51, 64, 71, 106
  indigenous people and, 94
  judicial branch, 58, 67–68, *68*, 70
  laws, 64, 66, 68
  legislative branch, 55, *62*, 66–67, *66*
  liberals, 50, 52–53, 54, 55, 56, 65
  local governments, 70
  military, 26, 55, 60, 65, 66, 94
  National Front, 55–56
  Plan Colombia, 59–60
  political parties, 65
  presidents, 12, 50, 54, *54*, 55, 57, 58, *58*, 61, 63–65, *65*, 69, *69*, 110
  Real Audiencia of Santa Fé de Bogotá, 45–46

Meet the Author

NEL YOMTOV IS AN AWARD-WINNING AUTHOR and editor with a passion for writing nonfiction books for young people. Bitten by the reading bug at an early age, he learned how books could be the doorway to the wonders of our world and its people. Writing gives him an opportunity to investigate the subjects he loves best and to share his discoveries with young readers. In recent years, he has written books about history and geography as well as graphic-novel adaptations of classic mythology, sports biographies, and science topics.

Yomtov was born in New York City. After graduating college, he worked at Marvel Comics, where he handled all phases of comic book production. By the time he left seven years later, he was supervisor of the product development division of Marvel's licensing program. Yomtov has also written, edited, and colored hundreds of Marvel comic books.

He has served as editorial director of a children's nonfiction book publisher and also as publisher of the Hammond World Atlas book division. In between, he squeezed in a two-year stint as consultant to Major League Baseball, where he helped supervise an educational program for elementary and middle schools throughout the country.

Yomtov lives in the New York area with his wife, Nancy, a teacher and writer, and son, Jess, a writer and radio broadcaster. He spends his leisure hours on the softball fields in New York City's Central Park and at neighborhood blues clubs playing harmonica with local bands.

Photo Credits

Photographs ©:

age fotostock: 103 top (Fotosearch RM), 45 (Rodrigo Montoya);

Alamy Images: 13 (Alex Segre), 80 (Aurora Photos), 119 bottom (Borderlands), 61 (Christian Kober 1), 96 (Danita Delimont), 7 top right, 118 (dbimages), 109 (epa european pressphoto agency b.v.), 103 bottom (Ferruccio), 48 right (Galit Seligmann), 81 (Guy Bell), 6 top center (Horizons WWP), 86 (Horizons WWP), 120 (imagebroker), 112 (James Quine), 84 (Jesse Kraft), 8 (LOOK Die Bildagentur der Fotografen GmbH), 21 (mediacolor's), cover (Roberto Orrú), 97 (Seb Agudelo), 100 (Stefano Paterna), 89 (Yaacov Dagan), 119 top (ZUMA Press, Inc.);

AP Images: 108 (Dario Lopez-Mills), 12 (Dolores Ochoa), 57 (Efrain Patino), 59, 65, 66 (Fernando Vergara), 82 (Fotolia), 19 (Ingeominas), 58 (J. Scott Applewhite), 64 bottom (Lino Chipana), 88 (Redacción eltiempo.com), 68, 70, 98, 101 (William Fernando Martinez), 55 (AP Images:);

Corbis Images: 113, 133 bottom (Henry Ruggeri);

Dreamstime: 64 top (Dawn Hudson), 131 top (Dawn Hudson), 34 (Edurivero), 29 right, 130 left (Ildipapp), 42 (Jenny37), 24, 36, 62 (Jesse Kraft), 102, 132 top (Kurtwilliams), 77, 132 bottom (Max Blain), 29 left (Noamfein), 125 (Uli Danner), 28 (Vladislav Galenko);

Getty Images: 114 (Adam Liebendorfer for The Washington Post), 2, 104 (Alfredo Maiquez), 17 (Bjorn Holland), 127 (Dan Herrick), 71 bottom right (Eitan Abramovich/AFP), 7 top left, 20 (Franck Guiziou), 53 (Hamilton Wright), 14 (Jane Sweeney), 5 (John Coletti), 126 (Jupiterimages), back cover, 6 top left, 25, 71 top right (Krzysztof Dydynski), 72 (Ligia Botero), 27, 60 (Luis Acosta/AFP), 11, 74 (Luis Robayo/AFP), 30, 83 (Margie Politzer), 44 top (Mauricio Duenas/AFP), 6 top right, 116 (Paul Kennedy), 56 (Pedro Ugarte/AFP), 115 (Phil Walter), 38 (Roger Smith), 26 (STR/AFP), 37 (Thomas Marent), 110 (Ulf Andersen), 35 right, 131 bottom (Veronique Durruty);

iStockphoto: 124 (Juanmonino);

Library of Congress: 54 (Library of Congress);

Newscom: 94 left, 94 right (JOBARD/SIPA);

Science Source: 33 (Frank Schreider);

Superstock, Inc.: 35 left (age fotostock), 69 (Album/Prisma), 39 (Animals Animals), 48 left (Blake Kent), 23 (Carlos Adolfo Sastoque N.), 18 (Christian Kober), 40 (DeAgostini), 92, 93 (Eye Ubiquitous), 106 (Franck Guiziou), 51 (Iberfoto), 76, 78, 85 (imagebroker.net), 123 (Jan Sochor), 16 left, 90 (John Warburton Lee), 32 (Minden Pictures), 107 (Rafael Campillo), 44 bottom (Robert Harding Picture Library), 121, 133 top (Ton Koene),

The Image Works: 46 (Mary Evans Picture Library), 52 (Mary Evans/Grenville Collins Postcard Collection);

Maps by XNR Productions, Inc.